I0113296

EAST KALIMANTAN
THE DECLINE OF A COMMERCIAL ARISTOCRACY

BURHAN DJABIER MAGENDA

EAST KALIMANTAN
THE DECLINE OF A COMMERCIAL ARISTOCRACY

EQUINOX
PUBLISHING
JAKARTA KUALA LUMPUR

Equinox Publishing (Asia) Pte Ltd
No 3. Shenton Way
#10-05 Shenton House
Singapore 068805

www.EquinoxPublishing.com

East Kalimantan: The Decline of a Commercial Aristocracy
by Burhan Djabier Magenda

ISBN 978-602-8397-21-6

First Equinox Edition 2010

Copyright © 1991 by Cornell Southeast Asia Program Publications;
renewed 2010.This is a reprint edition authorized by the original
publisher, Cornell Southeast Asia Program, Ithaca, New York.

Printed in the United States

1 3 5 7 9 10 8 6 4 2

All rights reserved. No part of this publication may be reproduced, stored in
a retrieval system, or transmitted in any form or by any means, electronic,
mechanical, photocopying, recording or otherwise without the prior
permission of Equinox Publishing.

Table of Contents

PREFACE

In recent studies of Indonesia's regional politics one important aspect has largely been neglected -- the role of the local aristocracies which dominated many of the regions outside Java from the precolonial period through to the formation of the independent Republic of Indonesia in 1949. In his work Burhan Magenda has begun to remedy this neglect. He has studied the aristocracies in various regions of the Outer Islands from the colonial period through into the New Order government of President Suharto. In covering their history he has examined the strategies used by the local aristocrats to survive and attempt to continue their domination of political power in their regions.

The focus of this present monograph is East Kalimantan, where the local aristocracy was commercial in nature, tracing its origin back to the establishment of a "spice trade" route in the sixteenth century. The decline in the nineteenth century of the main harbor principality of Borneo, Banjarmasin on the south coast, opened the way for other states on the island to play a greater role, in particular the sultanate of Kutai in eastern Borneo.

In the harbor principalities, the commercial aristocracies stood at the top of the social pyramid and dominated important positions in the states, from the Sultan down to lesser levels. Their main source of power was the wealth they acquired from their trading activities and their monopoly of force. As trade flourished, arms were easily purchased from the Western powers, and the mercenaries, hired by these aristocracies and using these arms, came to occupy the second stratum in the social structure -- in Kutai made up largely of Buginese adventurers.

The harbor principalities did not exercise actual authority over the interior people of Kalimantan, controlling only the market and contact with the outer world. The power base of the aristocracies of these commercial states also remained largely independent of the peoples of the interior, unreliant on the surplus agricultural accumulation there, since the harbor states could acquire wealth through their trade activities. This independence, however, did leave the aristocrats without any foundation of population support outside their own mercenaries and slaves.

After the Dutch consolidated their power during the nineteenth century the local commercial aristocracies of East Kalimantan granted Dutch companies oil concessions, and in return benefitted in terms of military protection and commissions. When the Netherlands expanded its bureaucracy into the Outer Islands in the 1910s, although many of the upper echelons were staffed by Javanese *priyayi*, Dutch colonial officials in East Kalimantan based appointments to the bureaucracy there more on the candidates' standing in the local aristocratic hierarchy than on their educational qualifications. This administrative corps thus became the bastion of the local aristocrats.

Because of its cooperation with the colonial power, in particular the close relationship of Kutai's Sultan Parikesit with the Dutch, it has been more difficult for East Kalimantan's aristocracy than for that of some other regions to continue its traditional role in the post-independence period. Nevertheless, members of the aristocracy continued to form an important part of the local bureaucracy which was transformed into the provincial civil service after the establishment of the unitary Indonesian state in early 1950, thereby maintaining the aristocrats' importance in, if not dominance of the local government. In the early 1960s the Kutai aristocracy lost much of its power at the hands of a coalition consisting mostly of Javanese officers and the Banjarese civilians who had led the Republican movement against the Dutch during the independence struggle. However, under the post-1965 New Order government of President Suharto, the aristocracy has made a partial recovery within the bureaucracy and the leadership of the officially sponsored centrally directed government party -- Golkar.

Burhan Magenda's well documented study opens a new perspective of fundamental importance to our understanding of both the past and current political and economic development of East Kalimantan and of its relationship with the central power in Jakarta. It provides an illuminating analysis of strategies by which members of the aristocracy have succeeded in surviving under widely varying conditions. Clearly, despite the challenges they have encountered over the past 45 years, these aristocrats have shown a surprising political resilience.

Audrey Kahin
Ithaca, August 1991

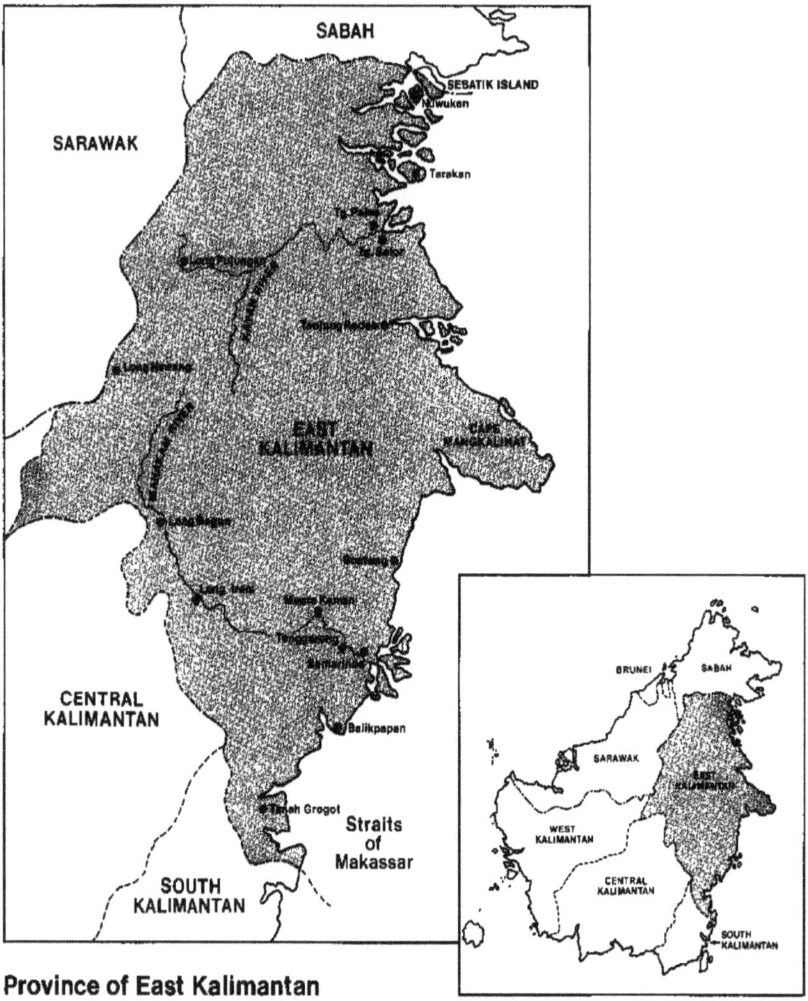

Map 1. Province of East Kalimantan. Source: *Indonesia*, no. 35 (1983).

CHAPTER ONE
GEOPOLITICS AND HISTORY

The province of East Kalimantan has a total land area of 221,400 square kilometers.[1] Approximately 80 percent of this, or about 17.3 million hectares, consists of forests. The Kapuas Hulu and Muller mountains physically separate East Kalimantan province from its neighbors on the island of Borneo, and largely preclude development of effective trans-regional communication. The province itself is extremely mountainous with low-lying land scarce and mostly located along the banks of rivers. Alluvial plains also form a narrow belt along the 500 miles of the East Kalimantan coast. Many small and large rivers originate in the mountainous interior. The profusion of mountains and rivers has had a marked impact on the distribution of the population and patterns of communication. The location of flat land primarily near the rivers has meant that the focus of settlement has been riverine. Moreover, because of the difficulties of traveling overland, rivers have provided the main, and sometimes only, line of communication between the various towns and human settlements of East Kalimantan. Indeed, to this day, almost no roads exist, the longest single road stretching only about 125 kilometers.[2] Hence, major towns and large settlements were established at the mouths of rivers navigable by large ships from the outside world. These river settlements later became the largest population centers in the whole province.[3] Accordingly, we find that the major towns of Samarinda,

---

1 For basic data on East Kalimantan, see M. Saleh Djaya, B. Sabran, and A. Moeis Ahmad, *Guide to East Kalimantan* (Samarinda: Yayasan Zamrud Nusantara Press, 1972), pp. 1-5.
2 A road was built between Samarinda and Balikpapan in 1980 and there will soon be a road connecting Samarinda to various places in the north.
3 The main centers of population are found along the Mahakam River, from Long Iram to Samarinda.

Tenggarong, Balikpapan, Tanah Grogot, Tanjung Redeb, and Rangjung Selor all lie at the mouths of long rivers which originate deep in the interior. (See Map 1, "Province of East Kalimantan," for the locations of important towns.)

Though it is easier to travel by river than by land, river communication is by no means always easy. An American explorer, William Krohn, noted in 1927 that "much of the course had to be chosen at the moment without any such tangible guide marking the way. As we shifted from one side of the river to the other, I thought we were simply doing so as the result of some inexplicable 'hunch' on the part of the captain. For example, I noticed that we always chose as the ship's course the side of the river where the nipa palms were growing on the bank to the very water's edge. It was explained that it was because the nipa palms grow only near deep water, so in following them as our guide we were in no danger of sandbars or mud-banks."[4] Moreover, it should be noted that river currents are quite strong for up-river sailing, and that most of the rivers of East Kalimantan are unnavigable.

Geography has also had its impact on the indigenous political system. Since human settlements were scattered, especially in the difficult terrain of the interior, it was hard for any single political entity to control the whole population. The so-called "Dayak" peoples were so divided along geographical and linguistic lines that their only commonality lay in their differences from the coastal Malays.[5]

The old kingdoms of East Kalimantan were situated near the river mouths. The oldest among them, the Kutai sultanate, was established late in the fifteenth century along the Mahakam River. Its first capital is believed to have been in the interior, at the site of the present-day town of Muara Muntai. It appears that the old Kutai sultanate was of the Hindu type, resembling the Majapahit sultanate in Java.[6] By the early sixteenth

---

4   See William O. Krohn, *In Borneo Jungles: Among the Dyak Headhunters* (Indianapolis: Bobbs-Merrill, 1927), pp. 74-75.

5   For studies on Dayak communities, see for example, Victor T. King, "Notes on Punan and Bukat in West Kalimantan," *Borneo Research Bulletin*, 6, 2 (1974); 39-42. See also Joseph Aaron Weinstock, "Land Tenure Practices of the Swidden Cultivators of Borneo" (MA thesis, Cornell University, 1979). See also, Carl L. Hoffman, "The 'Wild Punan' of Borneo: A Matter of Economics," in *The Real and Imagined Role of Culture in Development: Case Studies from Indonesia*, ed. Michael R. Dove (Honolulu: University of Hawaii Press, 1988), pp. 89-118.

6   See Aji Raden Djokoprawiro et al., "Sejarah Kesultanan Kutai," (typescript in author's possession),

century, the Kutai sultanate had its capital at the mouth of the Mahakam River, near the town of Samarinda. The relocation of the capital reflected changing circumstances within the old sultanate. Formerly, the sultanate had actually been a loose federation of many Dayak communities with a Malay *raja* at the top. The new Kutai sultanate, on the other hand, was a Malay sultanate par excellence, comparable to the many contemporaneous Malay sultanates in the coastal areas of Sumatra and Kalimantan.

Up to the nineteenth century, the Kutai sultanate's revenues mainly came from the taxes levied on forest products transported down the Mahakam River. The sultanate acted as a go-between in the forest products trade. The interior Dayak peoples actually collected the forest products which had come to play a vital role in the region's trade, and in return, the Kutai sultanate supplied the Dayaks with basic goods they needed, especially salt. The forest products were then sold for cash mainly to Buginese traders who at that time controlled the southern part of the Makassar Straits. In spite of its trade relations with the Buginese, the Kutai sultanate was not immune from attacks by the Sulu pirates, who dominated the northern part of the Makassar Straits prior to, and even after, the establishment of British rule in Sabah towards the middle of the nineteenth century.[7]

The Buginese formed the bulk of Kutai's armed forces. Upon their advice, the capital of Kutai was moved again in the seventeenth century to a new town, Tenggarong, about 30 miles up the Mahakam River from Samarinda.[8] By relocating the capital to the interior, the Kutai sultanate was able to prevent the Sulu pirates from taking over their kingdom as had happened to many small kingdoms in the northern part of East Kalimantan. Meanwhile, the Kutai sultanate continued in its role as a middleman in the forest products trade through the use of Buginese traders.

Beginning in the eighteenth century, and especially after the nineteenth century, there was a significant influx of Banjarese migrants to the Kutai

---

p. 20.

7   See James F. Warren, "Trade, Raid, Slave: The Socio Economic Patterns of the Sulu Zone, 1770-1898," (PhD dissertation, Australian National University, 1975), p. 23. Also J. H. Moor, *Notices of the Indian Archipelago* (London: CASS, 1967), and Reynaldo C. Ileto, "Magindanao, 1860-1888: The Career of Datu Uto Buayan" (Ithaca: Cornell University Southeast Asia Program, 1971).

8   See Djokoprawiro et al., "Sejarah," p. 16.

sultanate. This influx reached its peak after the dissolution of the Banjarese sultanate in 1886. Though large numbers of Banjarese also moved to the eastern coast of Sumatra and to the various parts of Java,[9] most Banjarese preferred to stay in Borneo, and so moved north. Many Banjarese settled along the Barito River in northern Borneo, and mixed with the Maanyan and Ngaju Dayaks. Still others settled at the mouths of the various rivers along the eastern coast of Borneo.

This influx of Banjarese migrants during the latter part of the nineteenth century had a considerable impact on the political landscape of the Kutai sultanate. Prior to the Banjarese influx, the sultanate had faced many difficulties in maintaining regular contacts with the Dayak peoples in the interior. The Banjarese migrants provided the help so badly needed by the sultanate to run its large domain. The Banjarese also settled along the Mahakam River, establishing small towns, bringing with them their skills in trade and organization. Indeed it was the Banjarese who established the small towns along the Mahakam River, from Samarinda to Long Iram. While most of the Banjarese engaged in trade activities, some were absorbed into the newly reorganized Kutai administration and became the Sultan's representatives in their newly established towns. Moreover, marriage between the Banjarese traders and the women of the Kutai aristocracy was common, facilitated by their similar Malay dialects. Only a very small portion of the Banjarese migrants, however, were incorporated into the Kutai administration. The majority of them remained completely outside the immediate control of the Sultan, and resided in the towns of Samarinda and Balikpapan.

In Samarinda, the former capital of the sultanate, the Banjarese built a new settlement across the Mahakam River from an old Buginese settlement. When the Dutch consolidated their power over the Kutai sultanate, Samarinda became the seat of the Dutch Resident for the whole East Kalimantan region. Not only did Samarinda come to have the largest population in East Kalimantan, but its administrative status

---

9 The Banjarese diaspora was to continue until the early twentieth century. On the east coast of Sumatra alone, the Banjarese numbered about 30,000 persons according to the 1930 census. See *Volkstelling 1930, Deel IV Sumatra* (Batavia: Landsdrukkerij, 1935). For an insightful analysis of Banjarmasin history, see Idwar Saleh, *Sedjara Bandjarmasin* (Bandung: Balai Pendidikan Guru, 1959). A large number of Banjarese also settled in Cianjur (West Java), Surabaya, and Lombok.

was eventually changed, coming under direct Dutch administrative rule. In time, Samarinda became a Banjarese city par excellence, outside the reach of the Kutai sultanate. Though many of the colonial offices recruited Samarinda's Banjarese as low-level officials once Samarinda became a Dutch administrative center, most Banjarese remained engaged in trade activities. In fact, the Banjarese became the dominant traders in the region, a position once occupied by the Buginese, who had now become sailors and fishermen. By virtue of their contacts in Java, the Banjarese of Samarinda were in time to become the educated elite of East Kalimantan, from which most of the bureaucracy's officials were to be recruited.

As stated previously, the other city with a large Banjarese population was Balikpapan. Prior to the end of the nineteenth century, Balikpapan was a small outpost for the Kutai sultanate, comparable to the many little coastal towns along the Makassar Straits. Since it was not connected to the resource-rich interior areas, its role was not that important. The discovery of oil at the end of the nineteenth century, however, radically altered its commercial significance, and Balikpapan quickly came to be the largest city in East Kalimantan. As with Samarinda, most of Balikpapan's population were Banjarese migrants who came early in the twentieth century. However, while the migrants to Samarinda were mainly middle and upper class individuals from around the region of Banjarmasin, most of the Banjarese settlers in Balikpapan came from the Hulu Sungai area, and worked as laborers in the oilfields. Whereas Banjarese migrants in Samarinda came to dominate trade in that city, only a few of the Banjarese migrants in Balikpapan were able to obtain administrative jobs connected to oil production. These differences in origins, occupational experiences, and class backgrounds had a far-reaching effect on the political development of the Banjarese communities in Balikpapan and Samarinda.

The discovery of oil also attracted a large number of Javanese laborers to East Kalimantan. They were brought in by the Dutch companies under contractual provisions and conditions similar to those imposed on the Javanese laborers used on the plantations of East Sumatra.[10]

---

10 For a good discussion of the experiences of the Javanese laborers in East Sumatran plantations, see William J. O'Malley, "Indonesia in the Great Depression: a Study of East Sumatra and Jogjakarta in the 1930s" (PhD dissertation, Cornell University, 1977)," pp. 104-43, and AJ.S. Reid, *The Blood of*

These Javanese laborers were not only present in the various oil-towns around Balikpapan, such as Semboja and Sanga-sanga, but were also concentrated in the city of Balikpapan itself. In addition to its Banjarese and Javanese inhabitants, Balikpapan also had its Buginese, Makassarese, and Minahassan communities. The oil industry was also the economic mainstay of these other ethnic communities. Thus, for example, while the Dutch dominated the upper echelon of the oil companies' hierarchy, the lower administrative staff was mostly Minahassan. Hence, Balikpapan's population was more ethnically heterogeneous than Samarinda's. Moreover, unlike Samarinda, all the various segments of the population in Balikpapan were tied in one way or another to the oil industry.

Unlike Samarinda, Balikpapan never became a city under direct Dutch rule. The Kutai sultanate kept Balikpapan under its control through the appointment of an assistant *wedana* (district chief) for the area. Despite this formal control, communication difficulties prevented the Sultans in Tenggarong from having effective control over Balikpapan's population. Moreover, the huge profits from their share of oil royalties encouraged the Sultans more or less to surrender Balikpapan into the hands of the oil companies as a sort of "extraterritorial" zone. Balikpapan's ambiguous position with regard to the Kutai sultanate is important in explaining the later emergence of a radical anti-sultanate movement among Balikpapan's educated elite.

Apart from Balikpapan, the oil industry built the key town of Tarakan. Tarakan is located offshore of the Bulungan region in the northern part of East Kalimantan. It not only houses many of the employees working the off-shore oil drills in the Makassar Straits, but also has become an important transit port for the region. Its population is composed of a mixture of Javanese laborers, Banjarese traders, and other outsiders. Its population has increased so dramatically over the past decades that in 1979 it became the third largest town in East Kalimantan, after Balikpapan and Samarinda, with a population of 40,000.[11]

Nevertheless, the large populations in the cities of Samarinda and

---

the People (Kuala Lumpur: Oxford University Press, 1979), p. 40. According to Reid, the number of Javanese laborers was about 240,000 in 1929.

11 In 1980, Tarakan was given special status as a *kotamadya administratif* (administrative city) with the power to govern itself while still under Bulungan's *bupati*.

Balikpapan make these two cities the most important political arenas for regional politics in East Kalimantan. The other East Kalimantan localities, with their own indigenous political systems, have always been in the background, due mostly to their small populations and their geographical isolation. For example, there were four small kingdoms in the early twentieth century, namely, Pasir, Gunung Tabur, Sambaliung, and Bulungan. Pasir was originally a Buginese outpost located near the border with South Kalimantan. Its population was mostly a mixture of Buginese and Banjarese traders, Bajau fishermen, and a few Arab merchants who intermixed with the local people. Pasir had traditionally been at the center of a territorial conflict between the Kutai sultanate, which claimed authority there with the help of some Buginese, and the Banjarese sultanate. Although Pasir had long been under the effective control of the Banjarese sultanate, the nineteenth century dissolution of the sultanate made Pasir an independent kingdom.[12]

---

12 Pasir had always been under the tripartite influence of the Buginese, the Banjarese, and the Kutai sultanate. Only after the consolidation of Dutch power was it given its own ruler. See, for example, Djokoprawiro et al., "Sejarah," p. 19 on the role of the Buginese in Pasir.

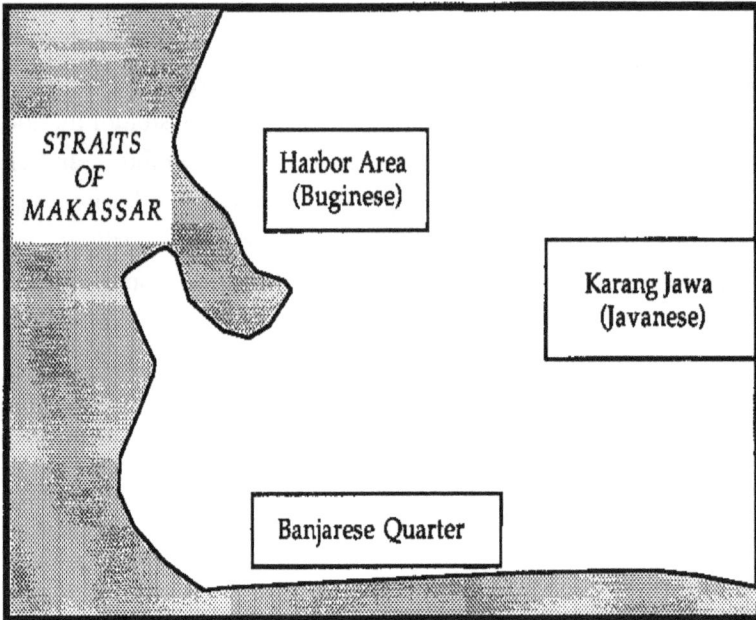

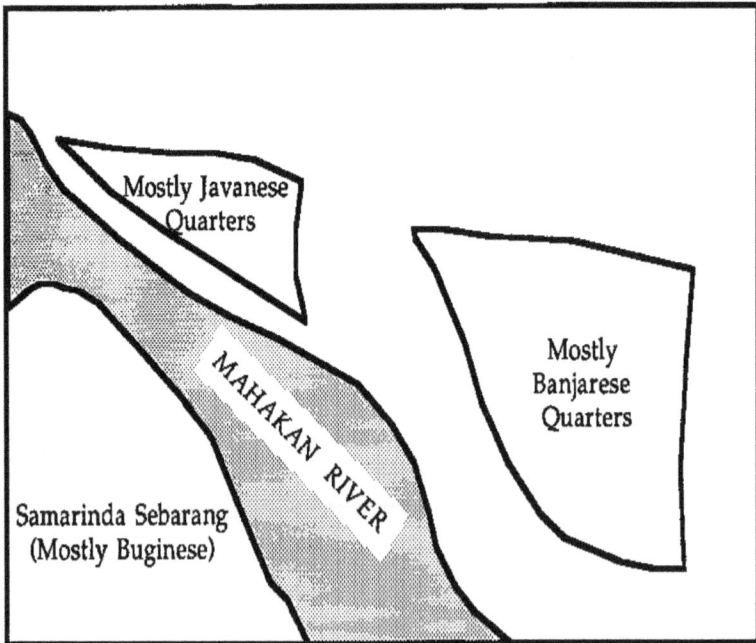

Map 2. Cities of Balikpapan and Samarinda

As was the case with Pasir, the sultanates of Gunung Tabur and Sambaliung were created by Malay traders who imposed their authority over the Dayak of the interior. The populations of these two sultanates were very small. In the early twentieth century, each kingdom had less than 5,000 people under its control. The Sultans lived from trade, sometimes by leasing trading monopolies to foreign merchants. It was in these two sultanates that a British merchant, William Lingard, established his own authority in the nineteenth century to an extent almost comparable to James Brooke's rule as the "White Rajah" of Sarawak. He was made a Pangeran (Prince) by the Sultans and was called the "Raja Laut Captain of Berau."[13] However, unlike James Brooke, Lingard's main interest was in the monopoly of trade, and not in the accomplishment of territorial rule. Hence, he was granted by the Sultans of Gunung Tabur and Sambaliung the monopoly over forest products and wax from 1863 to 1870.[14]

The condition of many kingdoms on the coast of East Borneo up to the middle of the nineteenth century has to be seen in the context of the trading and pirating activities prevalent in the Straits of Makassar during that period. Until the partition of Borneo between the British and the Dutch in 1892, and the agreement between the Spanish and the British in 1878 regarding the Sulu islands and North Borneo proper, the Straits of Makassar were full of pirates. Indeed, the situation in the Makassar Straits was comparable to the state of affairs in the Malacca Straits prior to the establishment of British rule in Singapore.

In the northern part of the straits, the Taosug from Jolo and Sulu were dominant up to the middle of the nineteenth century when they were defeated by the Spanish. There were also small kingdoms in the Bulungan region whose leaders consisted of Tidung Malays, Kenyah Dayaks, and Buginese chiefs and traders. These kingdoms were forced to pay tribute to the Sultan of Sulu who often raided them in order to gain control of the river entrances.[15]

Tarakan and Berau were the focal points of the trade that linked Kutai

---

13 See Warren, "Trade," p. 234.

14 Ibid., p. 236. For a more literary glimpse into the conditions prevalent in East Borneo during that period, see Joseph Conrad's two novels, **Lord Jim** and **An Outcast of the Islands** (London: John Grant, 1925). William Lingard's nephew, James Lingard, provided the inspiration for the creation of the main character of **Lord Jim**.

15 Warren, "Trade," p. 130.

and Sulawesi to Sulu. *Taosug perahu* came together in Tarakan before going to the mouth of the Bulungan, Sibuco, Sambakong, and Berau rivers. At the heart of Bulungan's trade with Sulu was sago and rice, as well as usual forest products such as wax, birds' nests, trepang, gold, and some saltpeter.[16] From other areas, such as the islands south of Sulawesi (Kalatoa and Tana Jampea), as well as from Flores, Komodo, and Sumba, the Taosug raided the surrounding indigenous communities and sold indigenous peoples as slaves to the Buginese traders.

The Illanun people of southern Mindanao were then also famous as pirates who sold slaves to Buginese traders from Batavia and Singapore in return for gunpowder. The Buginese traders themselves were known for their slaving activities. They raided the interior of South and Central Sulawesi in search of slaves for the growing markets of Batavia, Palembang, and Singapore.

Perhaps of equal importance to the slave trade was the role played by South Sulawesi's aristocracy who had set up many intermediary markets along the east coast of Borneo. The disintegration of many kingdoms in South Sulawesi after the coming to power of Bone's Aru Palakka around 1670 had forced many aristocrats to look outward for their financial sustenance. The aristocracy of Wajo especially came to depend on trading activities. They established many trading outposts on the eastern coast of Borneo where slaves came to be a key commodity.

When the Taosug eventually withdrew from the Bulungan and Berau areas, the Buginese filled the vacuum, especially in the latter half of the nineteenth century. Hence, while the Taosug from the Sulu sultanate continued to dominate the northern part of the Makassar Straits, the Buginese expanded their sphere of influence in the south. They controlled the entrance to the Mahakam River to such a degree that only after signing a treaty with the Dutch was the Kutai sultanate able to retrieve the powerful job of Samarinda's *syahbandar* (port master) from the Buginese *punggawa* (local ruler).[17]

---

16 Ibid., p. 119. In the year of 1843, about 20,000 people were involved in the procurement of trepang. Most of those involved in this enterprise were Bajau Laut.

17 For an introduction to Taosug society, see Thomas M. Kiefer, *The Tausug: Law and Violence in a Philippine Moslem Society* (New York: Rinehart and Winston, 1972). For the role of the Buginese in Kutai, see Warren, "Trade," p. 144. Kutai historians, on the other hand, tend to underplay the powerful role of the Buginese and to present them as being at the mercy of the Kutai Sultans. See

At the same time, the Sultans of Bulungan, Sambaliung, and Gunung Tabur were caught in the middle of the Buginese-Taosug rivalry. Accordingly, the three sultanates were sometimes tributary to the Buginese, sometimes to the Taosug, and occasionally relatively independent. To be sure, the Sultans of these petty kingdoms were by no means powerful. They could not even control events outside their own capitals, so that raids and counter-raids between Kenyah Dayaks and Tidung Malays over the birds' nest trade continued unabated for many years.

The trading enclaves of the Buginese and the Taosug on the eastern coast of Borneo were led by commercial aristocracies very much like those of the east coast of Sumatra. The character of these commercial aristocracies was best described by J. Zwager, who visited the Kutai sultanate in 1853 as a representative of the Netherlands East Indies government. He wrote that:[18]

Pangeran Perbala Sari, uncle of the Sultan of Kutai, resided in Muara Pahu. His job was to extract money with the help of his aides who were all opium addicts. Two other uncles of the Sultan, Pangeran Anum and Pangeran Raja Nata, rarely came to Tenggarong. They lived from monopolies and extortion.

He also reported at length on several cases involving the killing of traders on the orders of the aristocrats, who simply wanted to rob them of their money. His report also mentioned his difficulty in dealing with the Sultan of Gunung Tabur who "pirated all the perahu on the coast."[19] In fact, the Raja Muda of Gunung Tabur was even famous for his pirating activities within his own region. He was known for seizing everything he

---

Djokoprawiro et al., "Sejarah," pp. 16-17. It seems that Warren's observations regarding the role of the Buginese, however, are accurate, given the trends present in South Sulawesi's society at the beginning of the eighteenth century. The occupier of Samarinda was Aru Paneki of Wajo who was defeated by Arung Palakka and fled with his followers to Samarinda. After the installment of his man, Pua Adu as the *Syahbandar* of Samarinda, Paneki went back to Wajo to organize an alliance with Gowa against Bone.

18 See his report, translated into Indonesian, "Kerajaan Kutai di Pesisir Timur Kalimantan dan halihwalnya dalam tahun 1853," in **Sejarah Lokal di Indonesia**, ed. Taufik Abdullah (Yogyakarta: Gadja Mada University Press, 1979), pp. 61-104, at pp. 68-69. Zwager later became Assistant Resident for East Kalimantan.

19 Ibid., p. 81.

discovered, including even kitchen utensils.[20]

Thus up to the mid nineteenth century the region of the Straits of Makassar was marked by its instability and by the violent political competition between the Taosug and the Buginese. It was in this context that one has to see the coming of what Irwin called the "British speculators" to the island of Borneo. They were mostly traders who were able to persuade the local Sultans to grant them lands. Later, by obtaining monopolies over trade and mining activities, they achieved the position of "White Rajahs," such as Sir James Brooke in Sarawak.[21]

While William Lingard established himself as "Raja Laut" of Berau, another English trader, George Peacock King, had earlier been involved in business activities in Samarinda. The Sultan of Kutai offered him a monopoly over customs in Samarinda, which carried the monthly tax of 600 guilders. King refused the offer and, instead, got a concession for coal exploitation in 1853.[22]

Although the Dutch were well aware of the activities of the British traders on the eastern coast of Borneo, they could not do much to impose their own rule in that territory. For one thing, the Dutch did not have enough warships to control the troubled waters of the Makassar Straits. In his report to Batavia, the Dutch Assistant Resident for East Borneo, J. Zwager, wrote in 1853 that:[23]

> the Government had only one destroyer at its disposal which was stationed in Makassar. It was impossible to sail along the eastern coast of Borneo because of bad weather and insecurity, with that destroyer. The people of East Borneo did not see the presence of this destroyer as a protector for them. They felt no protection

---

20 Ibid., p. 83.
21 The best description of nineteenth century Borneo is still the one given in Graham Irwin, *Nineteenth Century Borneo: A Study in Diplomatic Rivalry* (The Hague: Nijhoff, 1955), especially pp. 191-214, on the partition of Borneo. For the history of James Brooke in Sarawak, see Robert M. Pringle, *Rajahs and Rebels: The Ibans of Sarawak Under Brooke Rule, 1841-1941* (Ithaca: Cornell University Press, 1970).
22 See Djokoprawiro et al., "Sejarah," p. 50. According to Warren, King was a Bengal-born Englishman who monopolized the rice trade of Lombok in the 1830s. He then established his headquarters in Samarinda and sent his agents to various parts of East Borneo in the 1850s. See Warren, "Trade," p. 234.
23 See Zwager, "Karajaon" in Abdullah, ed., *Sejarah*, p. 87.

whatsoever from the Government.

Beyond this, Zwager went on to say that, for the people on the eastern coast of Borneo, the name of James Brooke was quite popular. It was believed that, in the near future, James Brooke would travel inland from Sarawak to Kutai. There was confusion among the members of the Kutai sultanate as to whether or not they should welcome the possibility of a visit by Brooke. Although the sultanates of East Borneo were bound by the 1850 Treaty with the Dutch, the aristocrats believed that they would be in a better economic position if they tied themselves to a British ruler, such as James Brooke. Moreover, the presence of only one employee of the Dutch government underscored the feeling among the economically motivated aristocrats of Eastern Borneo that they were being neglected by Batavia.[24]

Though the Dutch were generally unable to stop the activities of the British traders, they did take decisive actions against William Lingard. When Lingard broadened his trade activities in Berau through the use of Arab and Buginese traders under his command, the Dutch sent *The Celebes* warship from Makassar to ensure that he would not become another James Brooke. (The son of Lingard's Arab associate, Sayid Abdullah Aldjufri, would take over Lingard's business in 1886.) Lingard's eventual departure from the region in the 1870s ended most British activities in East Borneo, to the delight of the Dutch who had just started to explore mining possibilities in that region.[25] However, it was not until the 1890s that the Dutch gave much attention to East Borneo.

By that time, the activities of the British traders in the Indonesian zone of the Malay archipelago had declined, and the famous trade route between Singapore-Banjarmasin-Lombok-Makassar and eastern Borneo had been reduced in importance by two developments. The first was the start of the Dutch consolidation of rule in the Outer Islands in the late 1890s and early 1900s. The Dutch used force, when necessary, to conquer the kingdoms of the Outer Islands. In a few instances, the Dutch had actually confronted some British traders who supported the local rulers,

---

24 Ibid.
25 See Warren, "Trade," pp. 236-43.

such as in the case of the kingdom of Selaparang in Lombok.[26] From this time onward, the Dutch, wanting other Western colonial powers to recognize their rule over the Netherlands East Indies, rigorously enforced the provisions of the formal treaties they had signed dividing the region into different spheres of influence.[27]

Because of these Dutch actions, the British had to order their traders to withdraw from the NEI territory. At the same time, the British had secured strategic positions in Southeast Asia, particularly with the growing importance of Singapore. In Borneo, they had also consolidated their rule both in Sarawak and North Borneo (Sabah).[28] It was the consolidation of British rule in Sabah through the North Borneo Charter Company that led to the phasing out of British interests in East Borneo.

Since the departure of Lingard from Berau in the 1870s and the end of King's coal concession in Kutai in the 1880s, the British had abandoned East Borneo. Instead, they concentrated their efforts in the newly acquired territories of Sabah where they built several trading posts. One of these posts, Tawao, was to become an important trading center with Dutch East Borneo, and it compensated the British for the loss of their former trading interests in the Berau, Bulungan, and Kutai areas.[29]

After their departure, the British traders were not replaced directly by the Dutch. Thus, there was a power vacuum in East Borneo's trade activities between the 1870s and the discovery of oil in 1902. It was a period of difficulty for the sultanates of East Borneo for they did not have much to offer to Western traders. Worse still, few Western traders and capitalists wanted to make investments in that region.

In spite of these difficulties, the shrewd Sultan of Kutai, Mohammad Sulaiman, was able to get some former Dutch officials to explore coal mining in Kutai. In 1888, a Dutch company, the Steenkolen Maatschappij Oost Borneo (SMO) got the right to exploit coal along the Mahakam

---

26 For the history of British and Dutch rivalry in Lombok, see Alfons van der Kraan, *Lombok: Conquest, Colonization and Under Development 1870-1940* (Singapore: Heineman Asia, 1980).

27 For an examination of the failure of Acehnese diplomacy, see Anthony Reid, *The Contest for North Sumatra: Aceh, the Netherlands and Britain, 1858-1898* (Kuala Lumpur: University of Malaya Press, 1969), pp. 119-55.

28 For the history of Sabah, see K. G. Tregonning, *A History of Modern Sabah, 1881-1963* (Kuala Lumpur: University of Malaya Press, 1967), especially pp. 4-30.

29 See Tregonning, *A History*, pp. 31-48.

River.[30] However, the various diseases suffered by the coal workers, and the decline of the sugar industry in Java caused this coal exploitation venture to fail. Eventually, this venture was closed in 1893 after its only ship was destroyed. The venture had lost about f. 800,000 by the time of its closing. It was later sold to another company, the Oost-Borneo Maatschappij (OBM).[31]

The failure of coal exploitation forced Sultan Sulaiman to offer still other opportunities to Western capitalists, aside from the traditional trade opportunities in forest products. Thus, for example, he tried to encourage coffee and tobacco plantations near Tenggarong. These plantation ventures, however, met with little success mainly because they could not compete with plantations in Java and East Sumatra which had lower costs of production. The higher cost-benefit ratio of production of the Tenggarong plantations was primarily due to the lack of an adequate local supply of labor and to the difficulties attached to the importation of Javanese workers.

However, luck was on the Sultan of Kutai's side, with the help of a Dutch engineer, J. H. Menten. Having failed to exploit coal in large quantities, Menten still believed that other minerals could be found in Kutai. In 1902 he succeeded in discovering oil in the Sanga-sanga field owned by the OBM. OBM then leased its oil exploration rights to a joint-company of British and Dutch stockholders, the Dutch Bataafsche Petroleum Maatschappij (BPM), and its oil marketing and distribution rights to the British Anglo-Saxon Petroleum Company.

The discovery of oil in Kutai, and later in Tarakan island in the region of Bulungan, was to change the history of East Borneo. The discovery of oil furnished the Kutai sultanate with the economic means through which it could maintain its position of dominance and wealth, not only in East Borneo, but also among the other kingdoms in the NEI. Moreover, this wealth enabled the commercial aristocracies to maintain their dynasties and power to a degree not previously known in Kutai history. Dutch

---

30 See Djokoprawiro et al., "Sejarah," p. 50. It seems that both in East Borneo and Sabah, coal was never to become economically important for the colonial rulers. For Sabah, see Tregonning, *A History*, p. 97.

31 Djokoprawiro et al., "Sejarah," pp. 51-52. In the forests of East Borneo malaria caused the death of 265 out of 888 workers in 1893. Ibid., p. 51.

protection eliminated the possible danger of outside attacks which had normally characterized the history of this commercial kingdom. Within the reorganized territory of the Dutch East Borneo residency, the Kutai sultanate was undoubtedly the leader of the many small kingdoms nearby. These lesser kingdoms received small subsidies from the sultanate in the form of oil royalties to support their status as commercial kingdoms.

This wealth also enabled the Kutai aristocracy to adopt the higher standard of living of the Europeans; thereby legitimizing the Kutai sultanate in the eyes of older kingdoms and aristocrats in Java and other parts of the NEI. From being a weak commercial aristocracy dependent on the protection of the Buginese *punggawa* and Taosug pirates, the Kutai aristocrats came to be very important Dutch subjects.

The discovery of oil also suddenly changed the Dutch attitude toward Kutai from one of benign neglect in the mid nineteenth century to one of considerable concern for an area now regarded as strategic in the early twentieth century. At a time when the Dutch administrators in Batavia were concerned about the high cost of maintaining the administrative unity of the NEI after having consolidated their rule in the Outer Islands, Kutai was to become a priceless prize. From then on, the history of East Borneo was to be seen by the Dutch as the history of Kutai, and especially of its oil. The emergence of oil exploration and production as the main activity in Kutai and East Borneo has generally shaped much of the history of the region and, particularly, the fate of the Kutai aristocracy.

CHAPTER TWO
OIL AND THE RISE OF KUTAI ARISTOCRACY

The modern founder of the Kutai sultanate was Sultan Mohammad Sulaiman who reigned from 1845 to 1899 before the discovery of oil. He had great talent in commercial activities, leasing out Kutai's lands for coal exploitation and plantation purposes. Since the Dutch at that time only exercised minimal control in East Borneo through the appointment of a political agent in Samarinda, Sultan Sulaiman more or less had a free hand in governing Kutai. Sultan Sulaiman worked so closely with the English traders that he had learned to speak the English language from them. He also took advantage of the presence of other merchants, such as the Arabs, in eastern Borneo.

Aside from the taxes collected by Samarinda's *syahbandar*, Sultan Sulaiman received various royalties from coal and plantation activities. Altogether, he was believed to have a monthly income of f. 60,000. The Kutai sultanate was absolutist in nature; most power was accumulated in the hands of the Sultans. Despite its monthly income from various types of businesses, the sultanate did not have a bureaucracy with any real power or regular salary. As in the commercial kingdom of Eastern Sumatra, power rested in the hands of the Sultan alone.[32] Hence, the distribution of patronage and favor depended solely on the Sultans' discretion. This was particularly true during the reign of Sultan Sulaiman, who only paid a regular salary to his *syahbandar*. The sultanate's other functionaries, including the Ministers, were paid irregularly according to the Sultan's mood or whim.

This power structure created two problems for the Kutai sultanate,

---

32 Djokoprawiro et al, "Sejarah," p. 56.

common to all the other commercial kingdoms. The first problem was the intense competition surrounding the process of succession. The spread of the practice of polygamy among the Sultans made the throne a source of struggle not only among the aristocracy, but also among the many sons of the Sultan. The lack of any definite rule for succession was not favored by the Dutch who later intervened directly in the succession decision, much to the benefit of the Sultan's sons.

The second problem was the arbitrary behavior of the aristocracy toward the other classes in Kutai society. Milner's description of the aristocracy's piracy against wealthy traders in a commercial kingdom provides an apt picture of aristocrat-merchant relations in Kutai, Berau, and Bulungan. In his report to the NEI government in Batavia, Zwager did not hide his anger and hostility toward the aristocracy of East Borneo who killed and robbed the traders. The fact that the aristocracy did not receive a regular salary legitimized this activity in the eyes of the Sultans, who sometimes took a portion of the aristocrats' profits.[33] As has been described by a Dutch missionary, Dr. A. W. Nieu, the power of the Sultans was of an economic rather than a political or religious nature.[34] By accumulating all the taxes and royalties in his own hands, the Sultan created a dependent aristocracy without any independent source of economic power.

Having discovered oil in East Borneo, it was in the ultimate interest of the Dutch to minimize the power of the Sultan and to make him financially dependent on them. In order to insure the flow of oil for their own benefit, they had to control the Kutai sultanate. The Dutch achieved this objective when the successor to Sultan Sulaiman was chosen.

The Dutch were able to reduce the power of the Sultan through the renewal of a political contract with the new Sultan. Although the Dutch had exerted formal control over Kutai ever since the reign of Sultan Mohammad Salahuddin in 1844, that control was not effectively administered on a daily basis until the discovery of oil in 1902. Dutch political control was aimed primarily at stopping the threat of British expansionism posed by their traders. Aside from King in Kutai, and

---

33 See Zwager, "Kerajaan," in Abdullah, ed., *Sejarah*, p. 71.
34 Quoted from J. R. Wertmann, "The Sultanate of Kutai: A Sketch of Traditional Political Structure," *Borneo Research Bulletin* (December 1971): 2.

Lingard in Berau, another English captain, Sir Edward Belcher, sailed his ship *HMS Samarang* along the coastal kingdoms of Gunung Tabur and Bulungan in 1845, and succeeded in getting letters from these Sultans agreeing to enter into a formal Treaty of Friendship and Commerce with Great Britain.[35] Accordingly, Sultan Sulaiman had considerable scope for attracting Western traders other than the Dutch. In reaction to this, and because of the requirements of the Cultivation System (*Cultuur Stelsel*) in the second half of the nineteenth century, the Dutch felt the need to exert pressure on the Kutai sultanate.

Their first political contract with the sultanate had been between a certain Major Muller, who represented Batavia, and Sultan Salahuddin of Kutai on August 8, 1825. It stipulated that the treaty was a friendship agreement requiring the Dutch to give protection to the Kutai sultanate and to provide an annual payment of f.8,000 to the sultanate in return for its agreement.[36] The Dutch at this time were more interested in controlling the flow of trade along the Mahakam River than in economically exploiting the Kutai sultanate.

The second treaty signed by the Dutch and the Kutai sultanate was related to a military assault launched by the Dutch in March 1844. Claiming that Sultan Salahuddin had arranged for a pirate attack by Kutai soldiers on a Belgian ship, *Le Charles*, two weeks before, the Dutch sent four war frigates from Makassar to Kutai as a punitive expeditionary force. Sultan Salahuddin refused to meet the leader of the expedition, Lieutenant Hooft. Instead, he retreated to Kota Bangun, a small town upriver on the Mahakam. The four Dutch warships then sailed to the capital of Kutai, Tenggarong, with about 190 soldiers. On April 6, 1844, they burned the old town of Tenggarong.[37] The Dutch attack on Tenggarong was also aimed at discouraging further contact between the Kutai sultanate and the various British traders active in the northern part of eastern Borneo.

The treaty of 1844 stipulated that the Dutch were the owners of the Kutai sultanate, and that this ownership "had to be recognized by the

---

35 See Captain Sir Edward Belcher, *Narrative of the Voyage of HMS Samarang*, Volume I (London: Pall Mall, 1970), pp. 236-37, for a reprint of the letter.

36 Djokoprawiro et al., "Sejarah," p. 23.

37 Ibid., pp. 29-34.

future Sultans."[38] The treaty also described the borders of the Kutai sultanate and the areas under its control. Beyond this, it provided that the Kutai sultanate was to be governed by a Resident in Banjarmasin. In 1846, the Dutch also started the practice of appointing an Assistant Resident for East Borneo in Samarinda, the first of these being H. Von Dewall.

When Sultan Salahuddin died in 1845, Sultan Sulaiman was still too young to rule so he was assisted by three ministers. In October 1850, the Dutch were able to extract a new treaty from the three ministers. While carefully preserving the borders of Kutai, this further reduced the power of the Sultan. The treaty stated that "the Dutch had given the Kutai sultanate to Sultan Sulaiman as a loan" and that all regulations from Batavia had to be implemented.[39] By appointing a young son of the deceased Sultan as the new Sultan, the Dutch gained the cooperation of the older ministers who were happy to govern Kutai until the young Sultan achieved maturity. A new treaty was drawn up in 1863 when Sultan Sulaiman took over the sultanate from the three ministers.

Under the 1863 treaty Sultan Sulaiman was required to assist the Dutch with manpower, gunpowder, and ships in case of war. It also stipulated that the Dutch would appoint then-own administrators in many parts of Kutai to whom the Kutai sultanate had to grant certain lands. With the activities of Lingard in Berau in mind, the treaty also stressed a prohibition against other foreigners acting as cultivators of the land in Kutai. The treaty, however, mainly stressed the dependent nature of the Sultan's rule over Kutai and the absolute loyalty he owed the Dutch.[40]

To summarize, despite his dealings with other Western traders, Sultan Sulaiman's rule had effectively been limited by the terms of the treaty. Moreover, under the treaty he was forced to help the Dutch fight their wars, including the Dutch war against the Banjarmasin sultanate in the 1860s. Not only did he provide soldiers for the Dutch, but he even led his own forces in attacking the retreating force of the Banjarmasin near Muara Tewe, in Central Borneo.

The discovery of coal in the nineteenth century opened up new economic opportunities for the Dutch, but required them to exercise

---

38 Ibid., p. 39.
39 Ibid., pp. 36-37.
40 Ibid., pp. 38-39.

tighter control over the Kutai sultanate as a precondition for effective exploitation of these resources. Upon the death of Sultan Sulaiman in December 1899, the Dutch appointed his eldest son, Pangeran Prabu, as the new Sultan, with the title Sultan Muhammad Alimuddin. The new Sultan had to sign another treaty in June 1900 in which the Kutai sultanate gave the Dutch certain rights over taxes. Among those taxes affected were the opium tax, the gambling tax, the Mahakam River transport tax, and the monopoly over the possession of arms.[41] By this time, the Assistant Resident working from Samarinda (Palaran) had effectively taken over control of Samarinda harbor.

When Sultan Alimuddin was to take over the Kutai sultanate formally in August 1902, the Dutch made him sign another treaty which for the first time provided for the forfeiture of some of Kutai's territory. The treaty also stipulated that the Ulu Mahakam (Upper Mahakam) district (*Onderafdeling*) was to be governed directly by the Dutch. For that right, the Dutch agreed to pay the Kutai sultanate f.6,000 per year. In 1907, the Dutch got the one square mile area of Samarinda that was to be governed directly as the center of government for the Assistant Residency of East Borneo. With the acquisition of Ulu Mahakam and Samarinda, the Dutch gained the ability to control traffic along the Mahakam River and thereby placed the Kutai sultanate under their military control. A company of the Dutch army was then stationed in Long Iram, the capital of the Ulu Mahakam district, while the Assistant Resident had his office in Samarinda.

The Dutch further weakened the Sultan's power by establishing a sultanate bureaucracy, which was staffed by Kutai aristocrats. The treaty with Sultan Alimuddin in 1902 had stipulated the establishment of a small cabinet for the Sultan. The cabinet had four members, responsible for justice, police, governmental, and financial affairs. The ministers, in fact, were half-brothers of the Sultan. By creating a permanent cabinet with specific functions, the Dutch minimized the possibility of quarrels among the sons of the old Sultan over the throne.

Moreover, the establishment of ministries and, later on, districts enabled middle-level members of the aristocracy to get involved in governmental

---

41 Ibid., p. 58.

affairs. The establishment of districts in Balikpapan, Jembayan, Muara Kelinjan, Muarapahu, and Melak in 1906, opened the way for middle and lower aristocrats to enter the sultanate bureaucracy. Some bureaucrats even came from non-aristocratic and non-Kutai backgrounds, and were given the aristocratic title of "Aji" by the Sultan.[42] It was from this group that the bureaucratic elite of the Kutai sultanate emerged. Possessing the proper educational training, this group came to dominate the daily affairs of the sultanate after the 1920s.

The emergence of this bureaucratic aristocracy was partly due to the reluctance of the immediate family of the Sultan to move out of Tenggarong. These family members were satisfied to work within Tenggarong's ministries since their ministerial positions allowed them to stay closer to the Sultan. Moreover, the presence of Dutch Controlleurs in the districts outside Tenggarong had put an end to the arbitrary abuses that had marked relations between aristocrats and commoners. Hence, from the economic point of view, it was better for the aristocrats to stay in Tenggarong where they could pursue an easy-going life, exemplified at its best by the Sultan himself.

The creation of a simple bureaucracy in Tenggarong required the separation of the sultanate's operational budget from the Sultan's own expenses. Under Sultan Sulaiman, all revenues had been concentrated in his hands. He had then distributed the salaries according to his own discretion. The Dutch changed this practice when they appointed Sultan Alimuddin. They gave the Sultan a fixed salary every month in the amount of f. 25,000, and also granted him 50 percent of the oil royalties and 10 percent of the royalties coming from forest products.[43] The rest of the royalties went to the sultanate's financial ministry to cover the expense of an ever-expanding bureaucracy.

The Sultan's salary was reduced further when Sultan Parikesit officially took over the position in 1920. When his father died in 1910 Parikesit was

---

42 Most of these bureaucrats were Banjarese officials of the Kutai sultanate who had married women from the Kutai aristocracy. The title "Aji" was reserved for people of high aristocratic background, either on the father's or the mother's side. There were three types of Aji titles: Aji Bambang, Aji Raden, and Aji Pangeran. The last of these was only given to sons of Sultans who were appointed as members of Kerapatan (Ministries). For a discussion of the nature of aristocratic titles, see Wertmann, "The Sultanate," p. 3.

43 Interview with Aji Bambang Abdurrachman, June 15, 1979.

only 15 years old and was studying at OSVIA in Serang, West Java. Between 1910 and 1920, while Parikesit finished his schooling, Kutai was governed by the brother of the late Sultan Alimuddin and Parikesit's uncle, Pangeran Mangkunegoro. Under Mangkunegoro, Kutai's bureaucracy was to gain a strong institutional foundation and considerable administrative expertise upon which Sultan Parikesit could depend. Perhaps most significantly, Mangkunegoro established a Dutch-medium elementary school, HIS, in Tenggarong, financed by the sultanate.

The bureaucracy built by Mangkunegoro functioned so well that when Parikesit assumed the sultanate in 1920 governmental affairs were the responsibility of the cabinet, including Mangkunegoro. From 1920 until 1940, Parikesit was aided by the cabinet members appointed during the reign of his father, the late Sultan Alimuddin. Hence, he was in a position not to worry much about governing his sultanate and could concentrate instead on leading an easy life. With the new treaty, the Dutch reduced the Sultan's salary from f.25,000 to f.7,000 per month.[44] However, he still got annual expenses of f.30,500 and a 5 percent royalty from the oil, coal, and forest concessions in Kutai. Aside from this income, the Sultan still owned lands in Bongan and Bengalon in the coastal areas of Kutai which furnished him with additional income from forest products. The Dutch also gave the cabinet and the Sultan f. 16,500 a year for the rights over the Upper Mahakam region and for the control of all taxes. All in all, Sultan Parikesit had more than f. 10,000 a month to spend, which made him one of the richest Sultans in the NEI.[45]

Since assuming office in 1920, Parikesit had broadened his private interests, acquiring expensive habits. He was known as a collector of cars, motorboats, and speedboats. Although he had graduated from OSVIA in Serang, he took little interest in governmental affairs. In view of this fact, Mangkunegoro objected to the Dutch proposal to send the young Sultan

---

44 Ibid. The reason behind the reduction was that Sultan Parikesit's salary was not to exceed the salary of the Dutch Governor General which was f. 12,000 per month.

45 See Djokoprawiro et al., "Sejarah," p. 64. In the late 1930s, the sultanate of Langkat in East Sumatra and the central government in Batavia had borrowed money from the Kutai sultanate, in the amount of f. 200,000 each. Interview with Aji Bambang Abdurachman, June 26, 1979. As a comparison, it should be noted that Parikesit's fellow OSVIA graduates only had a starting salary of f.50. For a more detailed discussion, see Sewaka, *Tjorat-Tjoret dari Djaman kedjaman* (Bandung: n. p., 1955), p. 13.

to the Indologie School in Leiden,[46] though he did go to the Netherlands in 1928 for the first of his many journeys.

The extravagance of Parikesit was such that an American scholar who visited Kutai in 1927 could not hide his surprise:[47]

> The furnishings of the palace surprised me, in that they were in no way indigenous to the jungle country or to the East Indies, but were all imported from Europe. Draperies, beds, canopies, tapestries, rugs, tables, chairs, clocks, candelbras, pictures and all the furnishings, were such as one sees in the magnificent palaces at Vienna and other continental capitals. The novelty and strangeness of the furnishings add to their splendor, thus more deeply impressing the people in this jungle country with the royalty of their sovereign.

On the indulgence of Sultan Parikesit in buying automobiles, Krohn wrote further:[48]

> He owns three cars, two of American make and one of European manufacture, any one of which would tickle the vanity of a war profiteer in the United States. But the Sultan lives in a country where there are no motor roads. His one thoroughfare is the Mahakam River, and that is best navigated by his beautiful yacht. There are several footpaths in his village, but no road fit for an automobile. There is, however, one narrow street about three-eighths of a mile in length. But this is too narrow to permit of turning a motor-car around in it. It is said that the Sultan orders out all three of his cars and first drives the full length of this three-eighths of a mile bumpy street and then, there being no room in which to turn the

---

46 Interview with Aji Bambang Abdurachman, June 26, 1979. It seems that by refusing the Dutch offer, Mangkunegoro could still rule Kutai while Parikesit was busy pursuing his hobbies. Upon his appointment as Sultan, Parikesit was to divorce his wife, a daughter of the *bupati* of Serang, and marry Mangkunegoro's daughter. Ibid. The tradition of sending the Sultan's sons to the Netherlands had been started by Sultan Sulaiman. He sent his son, Aji Raden Mangkuwidjojo, and his grandson, Aji Raden Atmogondowidjojo, to study the science of government in 1895. See Djokoprawiro et al., "Sejarah," p. 57.

47 See Krohn, *In Borneo*, pp. 117-18.

48 Ibid., p. 120.

car, he reverses gear and backs up to the starting point, stops, gets in his second car and repeats the dose, and does likewise with his third car.

Although Krohn's impression was a little exaggerated with regard to the availability of roads in Kutai, the luxurious life of Sultan Parikesit was well-known among the Sultans in the Dutch Indies. Members of his cabinet (Kerapatan Besar) got a monthly salary of f. 3,500 while lesser officials could get about f. 1,000 a month. In comparison with most aristocrats in the Dutch Indies, Kutai's aristocrats enjoyed a good life and high salary. While the sultanate could even afford to lend money to the central government of the NEI in Batavia and other sultanates in financial difficulties, the upper aristocrats in Kutai were also able to profit from the royalties the sultanates got from the oil concessions.[49]

It should also be remembered that in the 1920s, the actual number of upper aristocrats, those descended from the previous Sultans who had the title of Aji, were not that many. They were estimated to number less than 500 people, most of whom lived in Tenggarong. The top of the pyramid was comprised of the immediate family of the Sultan who got a monthly salary of more than f. 1,000 for each head of family.

The structure of the Kutai aristocracy itself was not very complicated. The Sultan was chosen from the sons of the previous Sultan and his *Permaisuri* (consort) -- formally, the Sultan could have four wives at one time in accordance with Muslim law. After the Dutch gained control, the new Sultan was always chosen from among the previous Sultan's sons who were still young, in order to minimize the new Sultan's power while he was coming of age. Thus, for example, Sultan Sulaiman was only seven years old when he was chosen as the new Sultan, while Sultan Parikesit was only fifteen years old.

Although a genealogical record exists of the Kutai sultanate from the sixteenth century on, a properly maintained record only started to be kept in the middle of the nineteenth century after Dutch protection had guaranteed the continuation of the Kutai dynasty. By the early twentieth century, belonging to the Sultan's family guaranteed a regular stipend and

---

49 Interview with Aji Pangeran Kertanegara, former member of Kutai's Ministries, June 20, 1979.

offered the possibility of a position in the newly created bureaucracy. The sultanate spent a total of f. 200,000 in monthly salaries, excluding the Sultan's salary which was paid directly by the Dutch.[50] The Kutai sultanate could easily manage to pay for its employees, even after 1910 when the Dutch further reduced the Sultan's share of royalties and revenues in a new treaty.[51]

Kutai's aristocracy was then, on the whole, a very financially dependent aristocracy. The aristocrats depended on the Sultan's patronage for their appointment to the various positions within the bureaucracy, especially since most of them had never attended any Dutch-medium school. Nonetheless, in the 1920s, recruitment among the aristocrats was determined by their education, especially at the level of District Heads (*Kepala Penjawat*) stationed outside Tenggarong. Although the Kutai sultanate had its own HIS in Tenggarong, further educational opportunities had to be pursued outside Kutai, either at OSVIA in Makassar, Serang, or Probolinggo, or at MULO in Banjarmasin.

The immediate family of Sultan Parikesit was reluctant to pursue further study outside Kutai, given the easy life they enjoyed at home. Moreover, the possibility of being stationed in a hostile environment in Balikpapan or Semboja, or in other district capitals, further discouraged them. The jobs in Tenggarong, although uninspiring, satisfied most of them. As a result, most students who went to OSVIA in Makassar were of middle aristocratic backgrounds. These middle aristocrats were the descendants of nineteenth century Sultans, and still had the right to use the title Aji. Their families, however, had intermarried with commoners and non-Kutais, mostly Banjarese and Arabs. It was they who later formed the backbone of the newly educated Kutai bureaucracy. Ironically, precisely because of their educational qualifications, the Dutch had appointed them to important bureaucratic positions, passing over higher aristocrats without similar educational credentials. Later all of these middle aristocrats were to play prominent roles in East Borneo politics. Included among them were persons such as Aji Raden Afloes, Aji Raden Sayid Mochsen, Aji Raden Djokoprawiro, Aji Raden Sayid Mohammad,

---

50 Ibid. Kertanegara was in charge of the Kutai sultanate's finances.
51 Various people in Samarinda confirmed the report that Pangeran Mangkunegoro brought special servants with him to carry money in trays while he shopped.

and Aji Raden Kariowiti.[52]

Aside from these middle aristocrats, there were two other groups of Kutai's aristocracy which would become important in later periods. Both the groups were made up of the Kutai sultanate's *abdi dalem* who were considered lower aristocracy. The first group originated from the Kutais who had served in the sultanate's army. They had been given the title of *Awang* and had their own quarter in Tenggarong, the Kampung Panji.[53] The second group was composed of the non-Kutai Malays who had aided various Sultans in their rule. They were given the right to use the title of *Encik Mas* and resided in the Kampung Melayu of Tenggarong.[54] (See Map 3.)

These two groups had also taken advantage of the educational opportunities offered by the Kutai sultanate. Since they did not threaten to exacerbate rivalry within the Kutai aristocracy, they were given important jobs by the Dutch, especially outside Tenggarong. Moreover, as a group they were able to maintain their position, because when the Kutai aristocracy came under attack they were not affected, because they were not considered part of that aristocracy.

At the same time while the Dayaks comprised about 40 percent of the population of the Kutai sultanate in the 1920s, they were not represented at the court in Tenggarong. The Sultan governed them indirectly through their own *adat* chiefs (*Kepala Adat*) who once a year came to Tenggarong to pay respect to the Sultan. Moreover, in Ulu Mahakam where the Dayaks constituted about 90 percent of the population, governmental affairs were in the hands of a Dutch Controlleur because of the region's status as a directly ruled area.[55]

---

52 For a brief biography of these individuals, see the entry in the biographical appendix to this monograph. See also, **Buku Daftar Riwayat Hidup Anggota MPR 1977** (Jakarta: Lembaga Pemilihan Umum, 1978), p. 670, for a brief biography of Aji Raden Sayid Mohammad.

53 See for example, A. Badaranie Abbas, "Pengaruh Faktor Lingkungan Terhadap Aspek-Aspek Tradisionil Dalam Birokrasi Kesultanan Kutai di Tenggarong," in **Dari Swapraja kekabupaten Kutai**, ed. Dr. Aslie Amin (Tenggarong: Pemda Kutai, 1975), p. 137. See also an interview with A.P. Kertanegara, June 20, 1979. According to Kertanegara, the *Awang* and *Encik* were the traditional inhabitants of each *kampung* and had no blood relationship to the Sultans. See also, Prajogo, "Stratifikasi Sosial di Tenggarong" (MA thesis, IKEP Malang, 1968), p. 40.

54 Prajogo, "Stratifikasi," p. 42.

55 According to the 1930 census, in the Ulu (Boven) Mahakam, the Dayaks constituted 86.9 percent of the population while in nearby Apokayan region, they formed about 99.60 percent of the population. See **Volkstelling 1930, Deel V Borneo en Celebes** (Batavia: Landsdrukkerij, 1936), p.

The Sultan controlled the Dayak chiefs mostly through the taxes that were imposed upon their forest products. The Sultan of Kutai never required Dayak manpower for his army, because in the old days, before Netherlands protection, the Sultans' own mercenaries were utilized in economic projects and pirate activities. To satisfy the Dayak chiefs, the Sultan conferred upon them various titles such as *Temenggung* and *Demang*. However, the granting of titles was "so indiscriminate that their prestige became grossly devaluated."[56] Moreover, various Dayak sub-groups never achieved important positions during the colonial period, mostly because they lacked educational opportunity. Although the Sultan formally opened the school at Tenggarong for Dayak students, only a few of them were given fellowships to enable them to study there.[57]

The Sultan of Kutai had also governed directly the Buginese in Samarinda Seberang ever since the middle of the nineteenth century. After the installation of a Dutch Assistant Resident in Palaran in 1846, the sultanate needed to insure that the Buginese would respect the agreement they had made with the Dutch. To this end, Sultan Sulaiman appointed a Banjarese police officer, Ince Miril, as his representative in Samarinda Seberang, with the title of *Pangeran Bendahara*, an appointment which the *punggawa* of the Buginese community, Pua Adu, saw as a threat to his own position. To enhance his authority over Pua Adu, Sultan Sulaiman dissolved the office of *punggawa* and in lieu of it, appointed many *Anreguru* (officials for security) and petty officials within the Buginese community; thereby facilitating the assimilation of the Buginese into Kutai society. The dissolution of the *punggawa* office had a deep effect on the well-being of the Buginese community as a whole. Sulaiman's actions effectively left the Buginese behind in Kutai's development; they have ever since constituted the lower class within Kutai society. However, some of those who were assimilated to Kutai and Banjarese society did achieve important positions.[58]

26.

56 See Wertmann, "The Sultanate," p. 3.

57 Among those who graduated from HIS Tenggarong, there was one individual who was supported by the Kutai sultanate to study at OSVIA Makassar. He was to become a member of the Kutai delegation to the Malino Conference. After converting to Islam, he adopted the name Sampan Zainuddin.

58 Only a few have become public figures, such as Rustam Hafidz, head of the political bureau in the

MAHAKAM RIVER

SULTAN'S COMPLEX

KAMPUNG MELAYU

KAMPUNG PANJI
(AWANG)

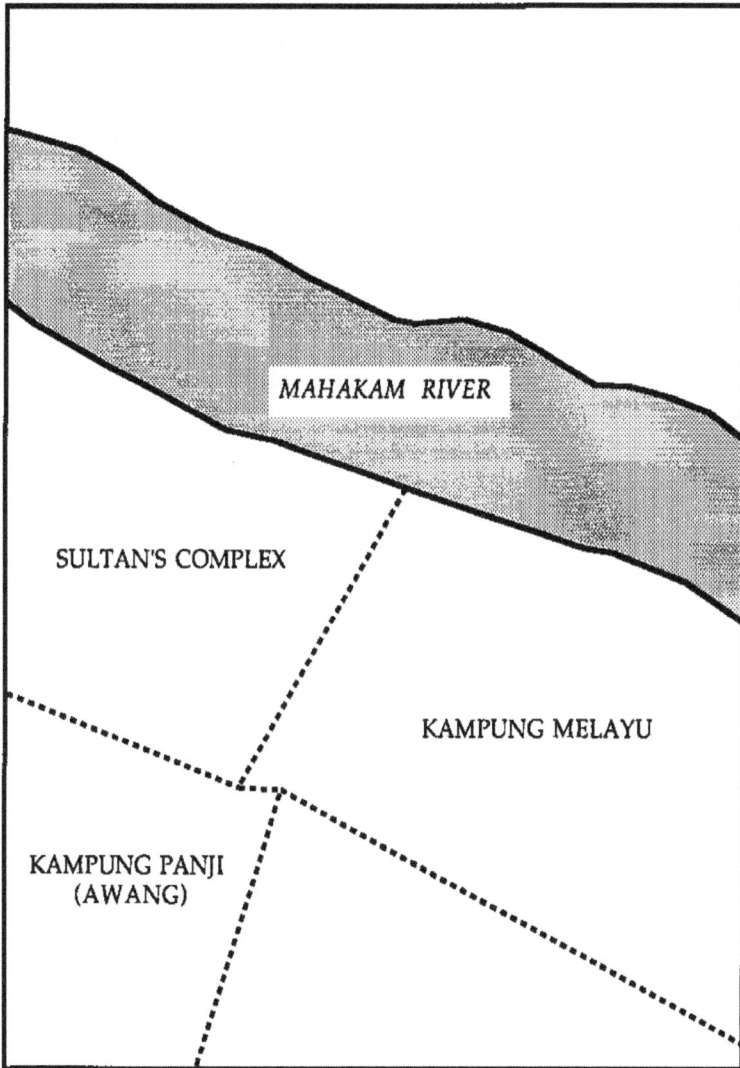

Map 3. City of Tenggarong

Governor's office who was proposed as a candidate for Mayor of Samarinda in 1979. The Buginese have achieved a more prominent role in Bulungan, where the Camat of Nunukan, Andi Achmad BA, is of Buginese descent. The first Bupati of Bulungan in 1959, Andi Tjatjo gelar Datu Mihardja, came from Bulungan and was of Buginese descent. In 1986, Rustam Hafidz was appointed as Bupati of Kutai, the most important position ever held by someone of Buginese descent.

The fate of the Buginese in Kutai differentiated the Kutai sultanate from its neighbors in the north, Berau and Bulungan. These two sultanates did not play a very important role in East Borneo's politics, mostly because they did not possess as much wealth as Kutai. Berau consisted of two small sultanates, Gunung Tabur and Sambaliung, which were the remnants of the old kingdoms of the days of *Lord Jim*. After the departure of William Lingard in the 1870s, Gunung Tabur and Sambaliung had declined in importance. Other than having Buginese trader outposts and Bajo fishermen communities, Berau had coal which was exploited by the Dutch for a brief period of time.

The coal was exploited by a Dutch company, SMP (Steenkolen Maatschappij Parapatan) in about 1911, but the reserves in Teluk Bayur were so small that it was soon abandoned. There was also an unsuccessful attempt to discover oil off-shore of Pulau Seudang in the 1930s. Because of its poor economic resources, Berau never played an important role in East Borneo's politics. In fact, part of the budgets of Sambaliung and Gunung Tabur were provided by the Kutai sultanate through the Dutch. While in the 1850s Gunung Tabur and Sambaliung could still depend on their royalties from forest products, the discovery of oil in Kutai and Bulungan left Berau behind economically.[59] The importance of trade in accumulating wealth had been replaced by oil royalties. Moreover, the departure of Lingard had discouraged trade activities in Berau, and Samarinda had emerged as the center of trade in the southern part of the

---

59 For a comparison, the figures below give a glimpse of the wealth of each autonomous region:

Annual Budget in 1857

Autonomous Region	Budget in Guilders
Sambauban	924 guilders
Pagatan	9,700 guilders
Pulau Laut	5,220 guilders
Pasir	40,557 guilders
Kutai	235,150 guilders
Sambaliung	45,057 guilders
Bulungan	55,080 guilders
Gunung Tabur	45,057 guilders

Source: *Politiek-verslag der Residence Zuid en Ooster Afdeeling van Borneo over het jaar 1860*, Book I.

Makassar Straits. The overall result was the economic eclipse of Berau by Kutai and Bulungan. The total population of the *onderafdeling* Berau in the 1930 census was a little more than 10,000 people, a figure which was less than the population of the emerging oil town of Tarakan off the coast of the Bulungan area.[60]

To the Dutch, the Bulungan sultanate was far more important than the Berau sultanate. As the melting pot of three ethnic groups -- the Buginese, the Kenyah-Kayan Dayaks, and the Sulu/Taosug -- Bulungan had provided a cushion between the Buginese and Taosug traders and pirates. The Taosug aristocrats (*datu*) dominated Bulungan up to 1860 as part of the Sulu sultanate. During these years of Taosug dominance, the Taosug *perahu* from Sulu rendezvoused at the island of Tarakan before they went to the interior of Bulungan to trade with the Tidung people.[61]

The treaty of 1878 between the British and the Spanish over the Sulu islands ended the influence of the Sulu sultanate over Bulungan. In 1881, the British North Borneo Chartered Company placed North Borneo (Sabah) under British jurisdiction, despite the Dutch refusal to recognize British jurisdiction in North Borneo. However, the Dutch recognized the British borders in 1915 after a long negotiation.[62]

By that time, the BPM had discovered oil off-shore of the islands of Bunyu and Tarakan. Moreover, Tawao on the British side of the border (Sibuco River) dominated the trade of inland Bulungan. The Kenyah Dayak and other interior groups were only too happy to cross the border and go to Tawao to trade. Bulungan's towns, such as Tanjung Palas and Tanjung Selor, had declined in importance.

Meanwhile, Tarakan had emerged as the center of oil activities and as the Dutch administrative capital for the Berau and Bulungan area. However, the Dutch had to pay royalties to the Sultan of Bulungan, who then resided at Tanjung Palas. Dutch protection and BPM's royalties sustained the Bulungan sultanate to the extent that it survived up to the abolition of the sultanates in 1959. It should be remembered that

---

60 According to Warren, in 1812, the sultanate of Gunung Tabur had a population of about 5,000 people. See Warren, "Trade," p. 150. In 1930, the census saw a population of 7,006 for Gunung Tabur, an increase of only 40 percent during the course of more than a century. See *Volkstelling Deel V*, p. 128.

61 See Warren, "Trade," pp. 146-47.

62 See Tregonning, *A History*, p. 23.

the Bulungan sultanate's power base was weaker than that of the Kutai sultanate, because it depended solely on Taosug support prior to the Dutch consolidation of power in the early twentieth century. Rivalry between the Kenyah, the Buginese, and the Taosug descendants was to continue, especially given the fact that oil royalties had strengthened the power of the Taosug Datu at the expense of the other groups.

While Bulungan was dependent on the sultanate of Sulu, the Pasir sultanate in the southern part of East Borneo was the domain of the Buginese. Formerly a Buginese trading outpost in the eighteenth century, Pasir became a sultanate under Dutch protection in the nineteenth century. Aside from its function as an outpost for traders between Makassar, Samarinda, and Pulau Laut, Pasir was of no immediate economic interest to the Dutch. The Pasir sultanate was maintained by the Dutch primarily to create a buffer kingdom between the Kutai sultanate and the Banjarmasin domain, from which the Dutch could manipulate either one of these two rival groups at any particular time. Like the Bulungan aristocracy, Pasir's aristocracy was a Dutch-created one which the Dutch used and manipulated in accordance with Dutch interests.

****

The nature of East Borneo's aristocracy, then, changed markedly after the discovery of coal and oil in the 1880s. Whereas before, it was merely a commercial aristocracy mainly composed of the descendants of pirates active in the Straits of Makassar, the consolidation of Dutch power formalized and institutionalized the aristocratic status and rank of its members.

Up to the 1870s, prior to the discovery of oil and coal, trade was at the center of the aristocrats' activities. They had established trade outposts for themselves in the small towns at the mouth of the rivers, populated by a few thousand people. They also had never shown any interest in land ownership and cultivation, although they were interested in the trade in forest products.

Intense rivalry and competition among the aristocrats over power and succession to the throne were quite usual, similar to the situation existing in East Sumatra's kingdoms as described by Milner. There was no rule of succession; ascension to the throne depended on the alliances and coalitions the aristocrats could forge. Slaves were not only a common source of labor in the region; but were an important trade commodity up to the abolition of slavery by the Dutch in the late nineteenth century.

The commercial aristocracy itself came from many different groups. In Kutai the aristocracy was Malay; in Bulungan it was a mixture of the Taosugs and the Buginese; in Pasir and Berau it was a combination of the Buginese, the Arabs, and the Malays. The Dayaks had always lived separately in the interior, although they did have important relations with these aristocrats.

The consolidation of Dutch power and the discovery of oil strengthened the position of these aristocrats. As had been the case in East Sumatra, the Dutch then found willing and important allies among these aristocrats. They not only gave highly lucrative concessions to the Dutch, but also relied on Dutch protection. The Dutch then instituted a quasi legal succession procedure through which they could further control the sultanates. Whereas before, the aristocrats had relied on private mercenaries to protect their status and interests from challenges from below, now the aristocrats rested at ease, convinced that Dutch rule in East Borneo and the presence of Dutch soldiers in the region would protect them from any populist challenge.

Moreover, the payment of oil royalties and Dutch subsidies to the non-oil sultanates, enabled the aristocrats to increase their standard of living and status to a level quite similar to that of the European landed aristocracy. The upper echelon of the aristocracy of Kutai and Bulungan, for example, could maintain a life-style higher than that of the Javanese Sultans. Though the origins and genealogy of their sultanates were unimpressive, the oil royalties had substituted for their poor dynastic background and had placed them in the forefront of the sultanates of the NEI. Their wealth alone placed them among the wealthiest of the Outer Island sultanates, such that intermarriages were sought between their daughters and the sons of the other wealthy East Borneo sultanates.[63]

---

63 For example, the daughter of the Sultan of Langkat was married to the son of the Sultan of Bulungan, while the Court Prince of Kutai, Parikesit married the daughter of the Bupati of Serang, Raden Ajeng Hasanah. However, the rule of succession fostered the intramarriage of the aristocracy, for it demanded that only sons of mothers originating within the Kutai aristocracy (pure blood sons -- *darah murni*) could be appointed as the new Sultans. Hence, the succession rule worked to prevent them from establishing strong family ties with powerful sultanates in

However, it was precisely these oil royalties which in the end put the aristocracy's future in jeopardy.

Java or elsewhere in the NEI. While the aristocrats of Kutai and Bulungan might have wanted to marry the daughters of Javanese bupati, their political future within Kutai would be endangered by doing so. The result was that such marriages were rare. In the end, this practice left them very vulnerable to the anti-aristocratic attacks of the period of "Guided Democracy" because they were left without any familial help from the other aristocracies in the NEI.

CHAPTER THREE
THE RISE OF TWO CITIES:
BALIKPAPAN AND SAMARINDA

The discovery of oil resulted in the emergence of centers for oil exploitation and production within the Kutai and Bulungan sultanates. While the Sultan maintained a handsome palace in Tenggarong, oil activity was centered in the town of Balikpapan, near the oil drilling sites in Sanga-sanga and Semboja.

Balikpapan stood on its own as the region's oil production center, geographically separated from the rest of the Kutai sultanate, especially its capital, Tenggarong. Prior to the twentieth century, Balikpapan had not played an important role in East Borneo's trade activities, as it was not located near any of the long rivers connecting the exterior with centers of forest products in the interior.[64] Hence, it could not function as a transshipment center for the trade in forest products as Samarinda, Tanjung Selor, and Tanjung Redeb did for the Kutai, Bulungan, and Berau sultanates. Prior to the consolidation of Dutch rule, then, Balikpapan was only a small village of mostly Buginese traders.

However, the discovery of oil in the Semboja area placed Balikpapan in an advantageous position. Only about 39 miles away from the oil fields Balikpapan was easily accessible by pipeline to them. Moreover, the BPM was eager to build its own port outside the control of the Kutai sultanate. Located within the well-protected Gulf of Balikpapan, Balikpapan was the best place the Dutch could choose to center their oil activities.

---

64 The longest river in Balikpapan is the Manggar River which is 19 kilometers long. There are no towns in its upper reaches. In comparison, the Mahakam River is 920 kilometers long. See **Desa Di Kalimantan Timur (Sektor Selatan)** (Samarinda: Akademi Pemerintahan Dalam Negeri, 1974), p. 10.

Although it was under the Kutai sultanate's jurisdiction, its lack of land communication effectively rendered Balikpapan a separate political-administrative entity. Hence, the BPM had a free hand in dealing with its oil business in Balikpapan, a town far from the Sultan's control.

The BPM soon built its own refinery in Balikpapan for the wells in Semboja and Sanga-sanga, and another refinery in Tarakan for the Tarakan and Bunyu wells. The NEI government, under the new concession amendment in 1918, got a high return from this oil exploitation, namely a 20 percent tax on oil profits, a 4 percent excise on the value of crude shipped, and a 20 percent tax on corporate profits.[65] Oil exploitation provided the NEI government with a sizable income, especially since the NEI only gave a fixed annual budget to the Kutai sultanate which owned the land under concession.

The growth of Balikpapan into a major oil city was to occur especially after 1910 when the joint Dutch and British Shell Company monopolized the production of oil in East Borneo at the expense of American companies. By 1921, the Nederlandsche Indische Aardolie Maatschappij (NIAM), a subsidiary of the Dutch and British Shell Company in which 50 percent of the shares were owned by the NEI government, was given the oil concessions in East Borneo.[66] The NEI government thereby gained a real stake in East Borneo's oil exploitation business centered in Balikpapan.

A rapidly expanding oil industry in the 1910s created various labor needs in Balikpapan. The first was the need for oil workers, which was largely met through the recruitment of surplus labor in the Javanese countryside that resulted from the Cultivation System (*Cultuur Stelsel*). It was not rare to find that contract laborers (*kuli kontrak*) were transported back and forth from Java to the plantations in East Sumatra before they finally landed in the oil fields of East Borneo.[67]

---

65 See Anderson G. Bartlett III et al., **Pertamina: Indonesian National Oil** (Tulsa: Amerasian Ltd., 1972), p. 47. See also J. S. Furnivall, **Netherlands India: A Study of Plural Economy** (Cambridge: Cambridge University Press, 1939), p. 328.

66 Bartlett III et al., **Pertamina**, p. 48.

67 Many of the Javanese laborers in Balikpapan had first worked in the East Sumatra plantations before being rotated to the oil fields in East Borneo. Interviews with various officials of Pertamina Unit IV, East Kalimantan, June 7 and 8, 1979 conducted in Balikpapan. See also interview with S. Mewengkang, June 28, 1979. For an account of the fate of the Javanese laborers in East Sumatra, see Ann Laura Stoler, *Capitalism and Confrontation in Sumatra's Plantation Belt, 1870-1979* (New Haven and London: Yale University Press, 1985), especially Chapter 2.

The number of oil laborers in Balikpapan alone was to reach about 2,000 persons before the Second World War. About 80 percent of these laborers were Javanese, creating their own Kampung Java in Balikpapan (see Map 2). They formed the bulk of the radicalized workers of Balikpapan during the Revolution and were to play an important political role thereafter.

The oil industry's skilled workers and technical staff in both Balikpapan and Tarakan, on the other hand, were mostly Minahassan. They formed about 75 percent of the staff positions (*kerani*), although their total population in Balikpapan was only about 668 persons. The rest of the *kerani* were Banjarese who mostly migrated from South Borneo in the first quarter of the twentieth century. It was from this *kerani* group that the leadership of the early political movements in Balikpapan emerged.

Although the oil industry directly employed less than 3,000 persons of the 39,092 people then living in Balikpapan,[68] the city itself depended on oil-created jobs. Balikpapan itself was not self-sufficient in terms of food production. It did not have an agricultural hinterland, and its soil was not fertile enough to be cultivated and planted with rice.[69] All consumer products from rice to meats had to be imported, giving rise to a vast network of jobs and distributional channels with the agricultural areas outside East Borneo. The Dutch, with the help of Chinese traders who had recently migrated to East Borneo, exploited this consumer goods dependency to the advantage of their commodities distribution company, Borsumij (Borneo Sumatra Maatschappij).

---

68 For the population of Balikpapan in 1930, see *Volkstelling, Deel V,* p. 127.

69 The soil in Balikpapan has a large percentage of sand. See *Monografi Kecamatan Tarakan* (Tarakan: Bappeda Kalimantan Timur, 1975), part I, page 11. Figures of rice land in East Kalimantan for 1976 are below:

Kutai	14,006	hectares
Berau	1,412	hectares
Bulungan	4,616	hectares
Pasir	6,875	hectares
Samarinda	2,815	hectares
Balikpapan	948	hectares

These figures are from *Statistik Daerah Tingkat I Kalimantan Timur, 1976* (Samarinda: Bappeda Kalimantan Timur, 1977), p. 64.

Table 1. Population of Balikpapan in 1930 according to ethnic group

	Number
Javanese	10,222
Banjarese	7,389
Buginese	1,951
Mandarese	610
Sundanese	805
Minahasan	668
Makassarese	526
Madurese	292
Kutais/Malays	52
Dayaks	32
Europeans	993
Chinese	4,427
Other Orientals	1,151
Others	9,974
Total	39,092

Source: ***Volkstelling 1930 Deel V Borneo en Celebes.***

Table 2. Population of Tarakan in 1930 according to ethnic group

Ethnic Group	Number
Javanese	4,082
Kutais/Malays	1,777
Banjarese	670
Minahasan	349
Makassarese	348
Sundanese	246
Buginese	237
Dayak	31
Others	1,841
European	567

Chinese	3,063
Other Orientals	197
Total	13,388

Source: *Volkstelling 1930 Deel V Borneo en Celebes.*

The role of the Chinese traders was quite important in the region's economy since they exerted a monopoly over the local distribution of consumer products. In the oil cities of Balikpapan and Tarakan Chinese numbered 4,427 (11.4 percent) and 3,063 (22.9 percent) of the total population, respectively (see Tables 1 and 2). The economic life of Balikpapan, in effect, was dominated by the Europeans and Chinese, working together at the expense of the Indonesian ethnic groups.

But although the Indonesian ethnic groups generally shared a subordinate position in the economy, they were by no means homogeneous in terms of the political or economic power they wielded. While the Javanese workers could not organize politically because of strong government controls and were weak economically because of their restrictive labor contracts with the Dutch, the Banjarese were in a better political and economic position. The Banjarese first migrated to East Borneo as part of the "Banjarese exodus" following the collapse of the Banjarmasin sultanate in the 1860s. Beyond this, the decline of rubber plantations in South Borneo in the 1920s significantly increased the number of Banjarese migrants to East Borneo prior to the Depression in the 1930s. Banjarese, known for their skills as traders and supported by a national network of Banjarese migrants, soon were able to compete with the Chinese in retailing and distributing consumer products to the urban oil centers in East Borneo. In particular, a sizable number of Banjarese settlers played an ever-increasing role in the economy there, using their *perahu* to transport rice and other food stuffs from the center of the rice-producing areas in Hulusungai.

Aside from the Banjarese, the Buginese also played a significant economic role in the region. They were active in the transport of food products (mainly beef) from the Pare-pare region to Balikpapan. However, unlike the Banjarese, they had neither the economic means nor political leadership to voice their grievances. Hence, it was the Banjarese who were to play an important leadership role in the political movements representing all the Indonesian ethnic groups. Later on, the Javanese and the Minahassans came to occupy important leadership roles in these political movements.

Their grievances were aimed at the Chinese traders and their Dutch protectors and, no less importantly, at the Kutai sultanate. It was the sultanate, and especially the Sultan, which came to provide a central frame of reference for nationalist opposition in Balikpapan. The nationalists not only resented the easy life of the Sultan and his family financed by the oil royalties, but also his careless attitude toward the welfare of his subjects, especially in Balikpapan.

While Samarinda was under direct Dutch rule, Balikpapan was still under the domain of the Sultan, represented by a *Kepala Penjawat* (Head of District). The *Kepala Penjawat* was supervised by a Dutch Controlleur as a civil servant of the *Onderafdeling* of South Kutai.[70] Hence, Balikpapan's population was still under an obligation to pay for Kutai's treaty liabilities with the Dutch. They had to pay a head-tax and to provide corvée labor for 24 days a year.[71] Since the Javanese workers and Minahassan professionals were on the BPM's payroll, the Sultan could not force them to fulfill their corvée labor obligations. Thus, the obligations of the Kutai sultanate had to be paid by the Banjarese who had no administrative ties to the BPM.

Moreover, the Sultan rarely used the Kutai sultanate's oil royalties to improve the welfare or living conditions of Balikpapan's population. While the sultanate built its own HIS in Tenggarong in 1913, and a few other primary schools afterwards, Balikpapan lagged far behind in the educational opportunities it offered. It was only in 1928 that it got an elementary vocational school, years after the sultanate had built higher-level schools in Tenggarong. For the majority of the people in Balikpapan, living conditions did not improve with the erection of Dutch oil industry facilities. The oil industry's professional staff lived in their own luxurious enclaves, with access to such modern amenities as hospitals and electrical and clean-water facilities.[72]

---

70 Abbas, "Pengaruh," p. 194.
71 Interview with Aji Bambang Abdurrachman, June 26, 1979. The amount to be paid by each head of family was 4 guilders a year.
72 Interview with Husein Jusuf, June 7, 1979. It was the Chinese company, Wang Phing Trading Co.

Furthermore, even though the Sultan extracted significant oil revenues from Balikpapan, and taxes and labor from its population, he never visited that city. In fact, Balikpapan was run by the Dutch Controlleur on behalf of the BPM. Having received his percentage of the oil royalties, the Sultan saw no need to visit this region of his sultanate. Formally, Balikpapan was under Kutai rule, but in reality it was an extra-territorial area under Dutch control. Conditions were thus ripe for the growth of a strong nationalist movement, especially among the Banjarese traders and Javanese workers.

Precisely because of its unique position, Balikpapan was to become one of the centers of the nationalist movement for East Borneo. Living in an industrial city with a sizable European population, Balikpapan's population received certain political rights from the Dutch without the consent of the Sultan of Kutai. Whereas in Tenggarong, for example, the Islamic *tabligh* had to get the Sultan's approval in advance, Balikpapan's population was quite free to organize political movements. Some wealthy Banjarese traders even gave financial support to these movements, both in Balikpapan and Samarinda.

By 1937, Balikpapan's political groups had had contacts with the nationalist movements in Java. Some prominent members of the national movements had visited the region, including such Gerindo (Gerakan Rakjat Indonesia) leaders as Adnan Kapau Gani and Adam Malik, who visited Balikpapan on their way to Samarinda in 1937 and 1939. While Gerindo had a branch in Samarinda, the moderate party Parindra (Partai Indonesia Raja) had branches in both cities. In Balikpapan, a Parindra branch office was established as early as 1933 by a nationalist leader, Achmad Nino Hadjarati, who was also prominent in the prewar nationalist movements in South Sulawesi.[73] By 1939, both in Samarinda and Balikpapan, the nationalist movements had advanced to the extent that they could form branches of Gapi (Gaboengan Politik Indonesia) and MIAI (Madjlisul Islamil a'la Indonesia).

---

which controlled the business of supplying the needs of the oil companies. See Syahbandi, et al., *Sejarah Kebangkitan Nasional Kalimantan Timur* (Samarinda: n.p., 1978), p. 39.

[73] Prior to and during the Japanese occupation, Hadjarati was one of the prominent members of the pergerakan movements in South Sulawesi. See La Sidek Daeng Tapala, *Sejarah Kebangkitan Nasional de Sulawesi Selatan* (Makassar: Departemen P. & K., 1977), p. 55. For his role in Balikpapan, see Syahbandi et al., "Sejarah," p. 43.

Prior to the Japanese occupation, then, the nationalist movement in Balikpapan had a strong anti-sultanate and anti-Dutch orientation, fed by the daily difficulties and frustrations that most Indonesians had to endure in that oil city and the realization that most Indonesians could only hope for a life of hardship under that regime. The feeling was especially strong among the Banjarese traders and retailers, who had to compete with the Dutch-supported Chinese, and the Javanese workers, who were without any organizational protection. Moreover, the different political conditions and economic arrangements and relationships in Balikpapan set the nationalist movement there organizationally and ideologically apart from the nationalist movement in Samarinda. Thus, Samarinda and Balikpapan emerged as two distinct and separate centers for the nationalist movements and political ideologies of East Borneo.

One of the most striking differences between Samarinda and Balikpapan lies in the composition and function of the Indonesian ethnic groups residing there. Whereas in Balikpapan, Kutai ethnic groups were largely absent, Samarinda's ethnic composition was quite different (see Table 3). The Banjarese were in the majority and constituted 54.93 percent of the indigenous population. Most of the first generation of Banjarese came directly to Samarinda from the Banjarmasin-Martapura complex of the old Banjarmasin sultanate. While they mostly had strong anti-Dutch feelings, they did not harbor as strong a sentiment against the sultanate as did Balikpapan's Banjarese.

For one thing, the Banjarese of Samarinda did not depend on the oil industry and were not subject to the taxing authority of the sultanate. Ever since the late nineteenth century, Samarinda had become the center of trade for forest products. Having gained a regular income from its oil concessions, the Kutai sultanate had given its rights to tax forest products to the Dutch authorities. The Banjarese had taken over the role played by the Buginese and Taosug, and came to play an important role in trade activities. Although they faced fierce competition from the Chinese, they were able to do quite well. In short, as traders, the Banjarese had fared better in Samarinda than in Balikpapan. At the same time, some had become administrative officials in the Dutch civil service and had been given important jobs such as *Kepala Penjawat* by the Dutch.

Table 3. Population of Samarinda in 1930 according to ethnic group

Ethnic Group	Number
Banjarese	4,620
Kutai/Malay	1,225
Javanese	1,167
Buginese	572
Bajo	257
Dayaks	30
Others	540
European	270
Chinese	2,201
Other Orientals	204
Total	11,086

Source: ***Volkstelling 1930 Deel V Borneo en Celebes***

Moreover, unlike Balikpapan, Samarinda was under direct Dutch rule and officially outside the sultanate's authority or jurisdiction. It was also the seat of the Assistant Resident for Kutai and Pasir[74] where many Dutch officials resided. As had been the case with cities elsewhere in the NEI, the population was relatively freer to exercise its political rights in Samarinda under direct Dutch rule than in Kutai under indirect Dutch rule. Finally, it should be noted that, whereas in Balikpapan the Banjarese did not even constitute an important educated elite, in Samarinda they dominated political life.

In contrast, the Kutais and the Buginese in Samarinda were not active in political movements because they were still connected in one way or another with the sultanate. Most of the Buginese worked as laborers in the harbor or in other low-wage, low-skill jobs. Similarly, most of the Javanese were engaged in low-paying occupations. A few Javanese were

---

74 For a description of the administrative divisions extant during the period of Dutch colonial rule, see Syahbandi et al., "Sejarah," p. 31.

technicians and professionals of the NEI administration, while the vast majority attempted to make a living as vegetable farmers and peasants. The peasantry was composed mostly of Javanese who had been encouraged to transmigrate by the Dutch in the 1930s. They were usually sent to Loak Ulu but the Dutch transmigration schemes there, as elsewhere, met with little success. In time these transmigrants moved on to Samarinda in search of farming opportunities.

Precisely because of its position as the center of administration for East Borneo, Samarinda had attracted many educated people of non-Banjarese origins. Most of them were nationalists who migrated to Samarinda because they considered it a haven for political activity. Horas Siregar, a journalist who moved from Pulau Laut to Samarinda and established a nationalist newspaper, *Panggilan Waktoe*, in 1933, is illustrative of this group of migrants.[75] Siregar soon came to lead a branch of Parindra in Samarinda, with the support of a Banjarese financier. In 1935, the local branch of PBI (Partai Buruh Indonesia) merged into Parindra, led by a Banjarese politician who had just come from Kotabaru, Roestam Effendi.[76] Parindra was to achieve considerable strength, so that in 1936 it was able to establish its own HIS. In 1937, the party's strength was further boosted by the visit of its leader from Jakarta, M. Husnie Thamrin who was also a member of the Volksraad. Consequently, Parindra was quite active in the prewar nationalist movements in East Borneo and was able to hold several public meetings in Samarinda, Sangkulirang, and Sanga-sanga.

Of equal importance to Parindra's organizational growth was its ability to attract young nationalists who had just graduated from the few elementary schools in Samarinda through its youth organization, Surya Wirawan. Indeed, the availability of an elementary education in Dutch-medium schools for Samarinda's children accounts in large measure for the very different place the nationalist movements occupied in Samarinda and Balikpapan, and the very different social basis available to the nationalist leadership in these two cities.

As early as 1923, the Dutch had established the HIS in Samarinda,

---

75 Ibid., p. 42.

76 The town of Kotabaru in Pulau Laut used to be a prosperous area due to coal mining done on that island. However, its coal-mining activities declined in the 1920s and Balikpapan was to attract many of Kotabaru's educated people. See ibid., p. 44.

attended mostly by Banjarese children. Moreover, Tenggarong was only four hours' sailing upriver from Samarinda. Road communication was also available between the two towns, making it possible for Banjarese children from Samarinda to attend many of the elementary schools funded by the sultanate in Tenggarong. A few Banjarese children were even accepted at the HIS Tenggarong, guaranteeing their fathers an income of more than f. 100 a month. But most Banjarese children attended elementary schools such as Teachers' Schools and *Vervolg* Schools.[77] The availability of educated Banjarese in Samarinda had made possible their appointment as lower officials not only in the Dutch administration, but also in Kutai's bureaucracy. They were mostly stationed in the interior towns of Kutai as *camat* (lesser officials), positions which had been refused by Kutai officials. In fact, the dominant position of the Banjarese migrants in interior towns such as Damai, Kota Bangun, Muara Kaman, and Muara Muntai was further strengthened with the influx of Banjarese traders who soon came to dominate retail trading along the Mahakam River. This influx of migrants was rather similar to the influx of the Banjarese along the Barito River to the interior of Central Borneo, following the collapse of the Banjarmasin sultanate at the end of the nineteenth century.[78]

Hence, the Banjarese of Samarinda had relationships with the Kutai sultanate to a degree that was not matched by the Banjarese of Balikpapan. While they resented the extravagant life-style of the sultanate's officials, they did not translate these grievances into personal attacks on the members of the sultanate's power structure. Rather, the Banjarese focused their attention on the institutional inadequacies of the sultanate. This institutional political orientation was further reinforced by the fact that many Banjarese intermarried with Kutai aristocrats. Hence, moderation always characterized the Samarinda Banjarese, while the Balikpapan Banjarese were in the forefront of those advocating radical solutions, especially with regard to the Kutai sultanate.

---

77 Ibid., p. 18, for the regulation regarding parents' income and the school entrance. For a discussion of educational policy in the NEI prior to the Second World War, see Christian Lambert Maria Penders, "Colonial Education Policy and Practice in Indonesia: 1900-1942" (PhD dissertation, The Australian National University, 1968), especially pp. 70-99.

78 The Banjarese diaspora to the upper reaches of the Barito River had led to ethnic conflict with the Dayak Ngaju. For this history, see Douglas Miles, *Cutlass and Crescent Moon: A Case Study in Social and Political Change in Outer Indonesia* (Sydney: University of Sydney, 1967), p. 104.

While Samarinda had a strong branch of Parinda, it also had a weaker branch of Gerindo. Led by Banjarese youths, Gerindo had a lesser status than Parinda. It was in Balikpapan that Gerindo did have a stronghold. Samarinda also had a strong branch of the Islamic movement, Penjadar, led by a former leader of Sarekat Islam, A. M. Sangadji, an Ambonese who had been exiled by the Dutch from Jakarta to Loak Ulu. Sangadji was a close friend of Sarekat Islam leaders, Oemar Tjokroaminoto and H. Agus Salim. Penjadar could be characterized as a cooperative political movement, especially when compared to the early Sarekat Islam with its radical stance vis-à-vis the Dutch.

Nevertheless, Sangadji was able to attract many followers within the Islamic community of the Samarinda-Loak Ulu complex. He was to become the focal point of young nationalists in Samarinda who felt that they were lucky to have a national leader as their adviser. Indeed, it was Penjadar which gave a significant political voice to Islamic politics and compensated for the weakness of other Islamic political movements in Samarinda, such as the Nahdhatul Ulama, Muhammadiyah, and Musyawarattunthalibun.[79]

The weakness of Islamic organizations in prewar East Borneo can be attributed to these organizations' orientation toward Banjarmasin. Whereas Gerindo, Penjadar, and Parindra established direct relationships with their headquarters in Jakarta, the Islamic organizations were branches of the Banjarmasin office. The effect of this organizational subordination was to prevent the Islamic leaders of East Borneo from directly linking and interacting meaningfully with the nationalist movements. Moreover, the absence in East Borneo of any Islamic schools (*pesantren* and *madrasah*) channeled the Banjarese children to Dutch-medium schools. Thus, although later on the post-independence Islamic parties showed a considerable presence in East Kalimantan's politics, their main basis of support was in the *pengajian* (religious activity) groups, and not in the *pesantren*.[80]

---

79 For the role of A.M. Sangadji in East Kalimantan, see Syahbandi et al., "Sejarah," pp. 50-51. In East Kalimantan, the branches of Muhammadiyah, Nahdhatul Ulama, and Musyawarattunthalibun were led from their regional offices in Banjarmasin. The latter was a Banjarmasin-based orthodox Sunni organization, founded in 1930 to counter the reformist Muhammadiyah. See Mohammad Taufik, "Perkembangan Muhammadiyah di Kalimantan Selatan dari 1925-1942" (MA thesis, IKIP Malang, 1972), p. 69.

80 In Kutai *kabupaten*, for example, there were about 27 *madrasah* in 1975, managed by several

Aside from Samarinda and Balikpapan, the nationalist movement had gained impetus in Tarakan where half of the population was Javanese. However, its geographical separation and the strict control maintained by the Dutch Assistant Resident there discouraged the emergence of any trend toward political activities. In addition, since Tarakan was entirely dependent on oil activities, the population did not have alternative economic resources for financing the nationalist movement, such as was provided by the independent traders of Balikpapan and Samarinda. Hence, Tarakan was never to develop a strong prewar nationalist movement, despite its large potential membership pool of Javanese workers.

Hence, the centers of anti-aristocratic feeling in East Borneo were in Balikpapan, followed by Samarinda. It was in these two cities that the two necessary elements for the emergence of a nationalist movement were present, namely an educated elite and an independent economic base. However, the ideological differences between the nationalist movements in these two cities, especially with regard to the position of the Kutai sultanate, had led the nationalists there to formulate two different approaches to the way of best dealing with East Borneo's aristocracy.

Islamic organizations and the government. Up to 1978 there were only three well-known *pesantren* in East Kalimantan. Two of them, in Tenggarong and Balikpapan, were founded by their Banjarese Bupati, with the support of government funds. The third one has been managed by the Pare-pare-based Darul Dakwah al Irsjad (DDI) which has established *madrasah* and *pesantren* as far away as Long Iram and Bulungan. See **Laporan Survey Keadaan Kehidupan Beragama dan Aliran-aliran Kepercayaan dikabupaten Kutai dan Pasir,** ed. Hamri Has (Samarinda: Fakultas Tarbiyah, IAIN Sunan Ampel Samarinda, 1975), especially pp. 22-49.

CHAPTER FOUR
THE MODERATES IN POWER AND THE SURVIVAL OF THE ARISTOCRACY

Their experiences during the Japanese occupation and, especially during the Revolution, further widened the differences between the Samarinda and Balikpapan nationalist movements. The radical position of the Balikpapan nationalists was strengthened by the military training provided by the Japanese, although that training only lasted a few months. It was in Balikpapan that the Japanese established their training center for youths from both Samarinda and Balikpapan. The recruits numbered about fifty and were given the task of guarding the important oil city alongside the Japanese army.[81]

But it was the Revolution which brought Balikpapan's youths to the forefront of the struggle (*perjuangan*). Balikpapan, which was the headquarters of the Japanese during their occupation, in 1945 became the headquarters of the Allied forces. Though the Japanese had improved the Sepinggan airport for use by their own Air Force, the Allies used it when they arrived from Tarakan in June 1945. These Allied forces were part of General MacArthur's command, and they took over the important oil installations in Tarakan and Balikpapan well ahead of British-led Allied forces entering Indonesia from Singapore.

Allied strategy made Balikpapan an important point of entry for further penetration into Indonesia, for it was there that arsenals and weaponry were accumulated for the movement of Allied forces into Indonesia, especially to Makassar and Banjarmasin. A sizable number

---

81 See Syahbandi et al., "Sejarah," p. 73. See also, Asnawi Musa, "Gejolak Revolusi 45 di Kalimantan Timur" (typescript).

of the Allied troops in Balikpapan were Australians, mostly draftees and many previously members of the governing Labor Party. Quite a few of these soldiers were sympathetic to the Indonesian Revolution, and from them the *pejuang* of Balikpapan not only obtained information about the independence struggle, but also weapons.[82]

Few though they were, the *pejuang* of Balikpapan had at their disposal sufficient arms to start guerrilla warfare when the Dutch KNIL [Koninklijk Nederlandsch Indisch Leger, Royal Netherlands Indies Army] returned a few months later. Balikpapan was among the first places the Dutch needed to control militarily, because of the importance of its oil fields and the presence of around a hundred Dutch nationals who were prisoners-of-war in the region. The necessity of gaining military control and of restarting oil-pumping operations put the Dutch in direct confrontation with armed *pemuda pejuang* (young fighters), aided now by about 50 deserters from the Dutch police force.[83] Among the *pejuang* there was a strong *semangat* (spirit) or conviction that the prewar status quo could not be allowed to be put back into place again by the Dutch.

The superiority of Dutch firepower made it difficult for the small bands of guerrillas to sustain their attacks. Moreover, the lack of communication and the low population density obliged the guerrillas to operate only in the villages near the towns. Sporadic attacks were initiated by the guerrillas in areas such as Semboja, Sanga-sanga, and Balikpapan. There was also a small guerrilla unit in Pasir which had been sent by Hasan Basri, Commandant of ALRI Divisi IV in Banjarmasin to assist the *pejuang* in East Borneo, under the command of a certain Abdurrachman,

---

82 Interview with Husein Jusuf, August 30, 1978. The Australian military also played a sympathetic role in Banjarmasin. Two Australian military leaders brought with them pamphlets about Indonesia's independence struggle and met with prominent leaders of the *pergerakan* (nationalist movement) in Banjarmasin. See Dhany Yustian, "Gerakan Rakyat Banjarmasin Dalam Menghadapi Pendudukan Belanda di Banjarmasin, 1945-1949" (MA thesis, IKIP Malang, 1976) pp. 64-68. It should be noted that the Australian troops which took Balikpapan, Tarakan, and Banjarmasin were under the command of Brigadier Sir Thomas Blarney. This 8th Australian brigade, in turn, was under the overall command of General MacArthur's Southwest Pacific Command of the Allied Forces which had earlier recaptured the Philippines. Only under the Potsdam Agreement was MacArthur prevented from taking over most of the NEI islands. For this interesting piece of Allied policy, and its impact on Indonesia's independence, see William Manchester, **American Caesar: Douglas MacArthur; 1880-1964** (Boston: Little, Brown, 1978), p. 429.

83 According to Asnawi Musa, about 50 police members went to the *pejuang* side, under the command of a Minahasan officer, Pangemanan. See Musa, "Gejolak," p. 5.

alias RM Noto Sunardi.[84] This unit never made it to Balikpapan and was crushed by the Dutch in Long Ikis, Pasir.

By March 1946, there was no further military threat to the Dutch from the *pejuang*. The KNIL had taken over control of Balikpapan and its oil installations, and had prepared the way for the political maneuverings required for the creation of a Dutch-controlled federation-type state in Borneo. Meanwhile, the *pejuang* of Balikpapan emphasized their experience of armed struggle against the Dutch, notwithstanding their small numbers and the short-lived nature of their struggle, using this experience to substantiate the claim that Balikpapan was "a city of struggle (*kota perjuangan*)."[85]

Aside from a short-lived armed struggle, the Balikpapan *pejuang* also organized a political movement of their own. This was made possible by the availability of a few educated leaders at the end of 1945. Prominent among them was Aminuddin Nata, a Banjarese who had graduated from HBS (Hoogere Burger School, Citizens High School) in Jakarta and had even enrolled at RHS (Law School) for a short period of time.[86] Another leader was a Minahasan, Siebold Mewengkang who had worked for the BPM as a middle level official in its accounting division.[87]

The first political movement to emerge from the armed struggle was named Komite Indonesia Merdeka (KIM), and was led by young groups of former Heiho (conscripted Indonesian laborers who were incorporated into the Japanese army). KIM was able to organize a mass demonstration on November 14, 1945, from which eager supporters for subsequent nationalist movements were recruited. Moreover, on November 29, 1945, a few days after the arrest of the leaders of KIM by the NICA (Netherlands

---

84 For the history of Abdurrachman Aziz alias RM Noto Sunardi, see Hassan Basri, *Kisah Gerilya Kalimantan* (Banjarmasin: Yayasan Lambung Mangkurat, 1961), p. 65. See also Musa, "Gejolak," p. 51, and *Sejarah Kodam IX Mulawarman*, p. 14.

85 The best-organized guerrilla unit was a platoon strength group, led by Herman Runturambi, a former policeman of Minahasan origin. His platoon took part in the recapture of Sanga-sanga Dalam on January 27, 1947. However, the guerrilla units were never to become a formidable opponent of the Dutch troops. Although some units continued to fight until the end of 1949, their military strength was negligible. See Musa, "Gejolak," pp. 75-82, for an account of the last campaign of the Dutch against the guerrillas, prior to the establishment of Federasi Kalimantan Timur.

86 For a brief biography, see Biographical Appendix at the end of this monograph.

87 For a brief biography, see Biographical Appendix at the end of this monograph.

Indies Civil Administration),[88] various leaders of the *pejuang* movements created a local front, Fonds Nasional Indonesia (Foni).

Foni was of a different character from KIM, especially in terms of its leadership. Whereas KIM had accommodated many young leaders with strong *semangat* for mass demonstration and armed struggle, Foni was mostly interested in developing a long-term political movement to support the Revolution. Its founders were Aminuddin Nata and Siebold Mewengkang. Having realized that the Dutch were increasingly capable of controlling Balikpapan militarily, they concentrated on politically organizing and consolidating the various groups within the Republican forces.

On June 5, 1946, when the Dutch had consolidated their control in East Borneo, Foni was reorganized as a party, Ikatan Nasional Indonesia (INI). It had its headquarters in Balikpapan, with Aminuddin Nata as chairman. It included many *pejuang* in its leadership, such as former KIM leaders Husein Jusuf and Tayib Kesuma. Siebold Mewengkang was to become the vice chairman and also the chairman of its affiliate labor organization for oil workers, Serikat Kaum Buruh (SKB).[89] The SKB was to become the forerunner of an independent oil workers' organization, Serikat Kaum Buruh Minyak (SKBM), still under Mewengkang's leadership, in the 1950s.

The momentum for INI's expansion came after the Malino Conference in July 1946. Republican forces in East Borneo had responded to the Dutch plan for the creation of a federal state by establishing INI branches in important towns. On August 6, 1946 INI had set up a branch in Tenggarong, to be followed in September by ones at Sanga-sanga and Melak, in November 1946 by ones at Tarakan and Muara Muntai, and in December 1946 by ones in Tanah Grogot, Samarinda, and Sangkulirang.[90] By January 1947, INI had branches in Berau as well.

INI's main aim was to insure that East Kalimantan be included as part of the Republic of Indonesia through mass action and other political activities. Its leaders had contacted the Republic's Governor of Kalimantan,

---

88 See Musa, "Gejolak," p. 42. See also in *Sejarah Singkat Kodam Mulawarman* (Balikpapan: Dinas Sejarah Kodam Mulawarman, 1975), pp. 8-9.
89 See Musa, "Gejolak," p. 42 and interview with Mewengkang, June 28, 1979.
90 Musa, "Gejolak," p. 42.

Pangeran Mohammad Noor, who was then directing the Republican efforts from Yogya.[91] Aminuddin Nata had traveled to Tenggarong in early July 1946, to persuade Sultan Parikesit not to send a delegation to the Malino Conference. He failed, and East Borneo was represented both at the Malino and Denpasar Conferences by its aristocrats, Aji Raden Afloes, Sampan Zainuddin, and Datu Muhammad.[92]

The KIM element within the INI leadership in Balikpapan was furious about the participation of East Borneo's aristocrats in the Malino Conference. They viewed this participation as the first step in an effort, fully backed by the Dutch, to return the aristocracy to power. In defiance of INI's formal position, they sponsored a series of mass meetings in Balikpapan and sent a telegram to Prime Minister Sutan Sjahrir that stated that "the Balikpapan people were behind the Yogya government and had nothing to do with the Denpasar Conference."[93]

Prior to the Denpasar Conference of December 18, 1946, Balikpapan was full of revolutionary spirit, activated by the young *pejuang* who were dissatisfied with the slowness of INI's leadership. Oil workers had joined the *pejuang* leaders in their activism, creating a crisis situation for the Dutch oil industry. The crisis was so serious that rumors were spread on December 10, 1946 that the feared "Zeven December" battalion of the Dutch KL would massacre all 2,000 oil workers in Balikpapan. This rumor was strengthened by the "Westerling Affairs" in South Sulawesi on December 11, 1946 which had intimidated anti-Dutch elements prior to the Denpasar Conference.[94]

The Dutch decided to wait until the end of the Denpasar Conference to arrest INI's leaders, partly because one of them, Mewengkang, was

---

91 During his appointment as the first Governor of Kalimantan, Ir. Pangeran Mohammad Noor had never come to visit the region under his administration. He stayed in Yogya and could not reside in Banjarmasin because of Dutch control over that city. He was to become the focal point of the Banjarese Republicans in their struggle against the Dutch. For a brief biography, see Biographical Appendix and **Buku MPR 1977**, p. 64.

92 For a complete list of the prominent aristocrats who attended the Malino Conference, see Henri J. H. Alers, **Om Een Rode of Groene Merdeka: Tien Jaren Binnenlandse Politiek Indonesië 1943-1953** (Eindhoven: Vulkaan, 1956), p. 138. See also, interview with Aji Raden Djokoprawiro, July 7, 1979, Malang. According to him, he was elected by the Dewan Kalimantan Timur to go to the Denpasar Conference. However, he was prevented from so doing by the Dutch who at that time doubted that the Borneo state would be created.

93 See Musa, "Gejolak," p. 44.

94 Ibid., p. 73.

attending the conference as an observer. Finally, the Dutch arrested prominent INI leaders in Balikpapan and Samarinda on January 24, 1947. Among those arrested in Balikpapan were Aminuddin Nata, Mewengkang, Djamaluddin Jusuf (a leader of Balikpapan's *pejuang*), and Mas Sarman (vice chairman of INI); while in Samarinda, the list embraced all the radical Republican leaders, including Djunaid Sanusi, Harun Nafsi, Mrs. Suwito, R. P. Juwono, and Sandijo.[95]

The effect of this mass arrest was to leave Balikpapan's Republicans without any leadership. The *pejuang* had lost their armed struggle because of Dutch military superiority, while the political organization, forced to continue without armed support, disintegrated due to the lack of leadership. Moreover, by that time, the Dutch had been able to impose their own political solution through the creation of the East Kalimantan Federation in February 1947.[96] Nevertheless, Balikpapan's *pejuang* refused to recognize this federation because of the terms and conditions this new political entity entailed. As a result, the Balikpapan *pejuang* were not represented in the federation, to the advantage of their rivals, the Samarinda leadership of INI.

Samarinda's fate during the Japanese occupation had been significantly different from that of Balikpapan. First, Samarinda benefited during the occupation from its non-oil activities. The Japanese did not impose strict military control on Samarinda, and continued to take advantage of Samarinda's function as a forest products' harbor. Prior to the war, the Japanese had their own timber concession in Sangkulirang which continued operating during the war.[97] Hence, in Samarinda, the Japanese presence was represented by people who had resided there during the prewar period, whereas in Balikpapan, the Japanese militarily occupied the city in order to control the flow of oil.

Second, the Japanese had been aided in Samarinda by the Islamic leader, A. M. Sangaji who worked with their administration as its religious adviser. Sangaji campaigned tirelessly throughout Samarinda, Loak Ulu,

---

95 Ibid., pp. 80-81.

96 See Alers, *Om Een*, p. 153. See also A. Arthur Schiller, *The Formation of Federal Indonesia, 1945-1949* (The Hague: Van Hoeve, 1955), p. 185 and *Republik Indonesia: Propinsi Kalimantan* (Jakarta: Kementerian Penerangan RI, 1954), p. 41.

97 The concession was in Sangkulirang, Kutai, and the rights were owned by a company under the name of "Nanyo Ringyo Kabushiki Kaysha" (NRKK). See Syahbandi et al., "Sejarah," p. 55.

and Sangkulirang, especially when the Japanese wanted to persuade the people to send their sons to be trained as Heiho in Balikpapan, at the end of 1944.

At the end of their occupation, it was thought that the Japanese were planning a massacre of the Indonesian educated elite in Samarinda, as they had done in West Borneo.[98] They did kill several Dutch administrators, but no massacre of Indonesians materialized. The educated elite became the focal point of Samarinda nationalist political movements following independence. Their principal leader was a Javanese medical doctor, Dr. Suwadji, supported mostly by Javanese and Banjarese nationalists.[99]

Under his chairmanship, Dr. Suwadji formed a committee to defend Indonesia's independence, known later as "Gerakan Dokter Suwadji" (the movement of Dr. Suwadji). He was assisted by several Banjarese youths, including Badrun Arief, Oemar Dachlan, and Djunaid Amin. Because of his activities, the Dutch transferred him from his Samarinda post to a small town in the interior in November 1945. However, his political work was furthered by another Javanese leader, R. P. Juwono who merged all independent movements in Samarinda into a para-military organization, Barisan Pemberontakan Rakyat Indonesia (BPRI).[100]

BPRI was quite different from Suwadji's movement in that it also incorporated many *lasykar* (militias) from around Samarinda. Juwono's assistants, such as Djunaid Sanusi and Harun Nafsi, were young *pejuang* of Banjarese origins. They established contacts with similar *lasykar* such as Barisan Sedewa in Samarinda, Banteng Indonesia in Tenggarong, and another BPRI, Barisan Pembela Rakyat Indonesia, in Sanga-sanga.

As was the case in Balikpapan, many *lasykar* were short-lived in Samarinda. The KNIL in Samarinda were harsher than their colleagues in Balikpapan. Soon, most of the *lasykar* had to retreat into the interior where the Dutch never pursued them, so that *pejuang* "hit and run" operations continued until the Round Table Conference in The Hague in 1949.[101] The Dutch were able to crush the Republican movements,

---

98 For an account of the massacre of the Indonesian elites in West Borneo, see **Republik Indonesia: Propinsi Kalimantan**, pp. 108-11. It is estimated that about a thousand Indonesian leaders, many of them doctors, were killed by the Japanese in 1943.

99 See Musa, "Gejolak," p. 39.

100 Ibid., p. 40.

101 The guerrilla units of *pejuang* were incorporated as a new battalion, Battalion C of the Infantry

mostly through arresting their leaders, or, as in the case of Dr. Suwadji of Samarinda and Dr. Suwondo of Tenggarong, simply removing them to unimportant places.[102]

The Samarinda branch of INI was established only in December 1946, long after INI had been formed in Balikpapan. Moreover, Samarinda's leadership was not involved in the Samarinda-based *lasykar*, BPRI. Headed by a Banjarese, Abdul Muis Hassan, INI Samarinda had its own different political strategy for the Republicans in East Borneo.

INI's members realized that the *lasykar* were no match for the Dutch army, and saw no hope in pursuing the military struggle. Having observed Indonesia's independence movement, they believed that East Borneo's fate would depend on events elsewhere, especially in Java. Moreover, they did not harbor particular resentment against the sultanate itself, aside from the fact that it was a dependency of the Dutch. In short, they tried to make the best of the difficult situation posed to the Republicans in East Borneo, always true to Samarinda's commitment to moderation. Whereas Balikpapan's *lasykar* and *pejuang* were mostly Banjarese and Javanese, Samarinda's moderates were mostly Banjarese, with a few Melayus. The local INI's vice-chairman was a Samarinda-Melayu, Inche Abdul Muis, who had just come back in 1947 from attending a university in Japan.[103]

The arrest of prominent leaders of INI in Balikpapan moved INI's political initiatives and leadership to Samarinda. By February 1947, the Dutch had succeeded in persuading the aristocrats to support the creation of the East Borneo Federation (Federasi Kalimantan Timur), which was to consist of the four *swapraja* (self-governing territories):[104]

Regiment of East Kalimantan, on December 14, 1949, by Lieutenant Colonel Sukanda Bratamenggala as a delegate from Army Headquarters. See *Sejarah Kodam Mulawarman*, pp. 18-19.

102 Dr. Suwondo was removed to Palu, Central Sulawesi, after years of service in East Kalimantan, including service in Long Iram. He was to become the Deputy Governor of Jakarta, between 1966 and 1977, when he retired. Later in 1977, he was active as the chairman of the PDI in the Jakarta region. Moreover, he became the PDI representative at the MPR in 1978 until his death in 1979. Dr. Suwadji became a lecturer at the University of Indonesia in Jakarta where he subsequently pursued a quiet teaching career.

103 For a brief biography of Inche Abdul Muis, see Biographical Appendix and *Buku MPR 1977*, p. 991.

104 See Schiller, *The Formation*, pp. 185-86. For an explanation of the significance of the autonomous region within the governmental structure of NEI, and Indonesia, see Usep Ranuwidjaja, *Swapradja: Sekarang dan dihari Kemudian* (Jakarta: Djambatan, 1955), pp. 41-42 on East Borneo.

Kutai, Sambaliung, Gunung Tabur, and Bulungan. Pasir was included for a short time, but was later transferred to the Southeast Borneo Federation (Federasi Kalimantan Tenggara) with its capital in Kotabaru.[105]

The return of the Dutch meant also the return of the old days for East Borneo's aristocrats. The Kutai and Bulungan Sultans were to have their own oil royalties again and Sultan Parikesit was also appointed as chairman of the Federation. The Federation had its own executive office, headed by a pro-Republican Kutai aristocrat, Aji Raden Afloes. The appointment of Afloes persuaded the Samarinda INI leadership to attempt to cooperate with the federal scheme. They also received a green-light from Governor Pangeran Noor in Yogya, who urged fellow Republicans in Borneo to enter various *Dewan* (councils) in their respective regions, with the ultimate aim of preventing the establishment of a Borneo State.[106]

The decision by Samarinda Republicans to enter the East Borneo Council was not surprising, given the fact that many Republicans had done the same thing in the East Indonesian State (NIT), and later on, in Dewan Banjar in Banjarmasin.[107] They had also succeeded in putting forward the candidacy of Sultan Parikesit as a potential first president or *Walinegara* (State Head) of Negara Borneo. Parikesit was nominated as *Walinegara* of Borneo partly because his half-brother Aji Pangeran Pranoto was pro-Republican and partly in order to counter the candidacy of pro-Dutch Sultan Hamid Algadrie II of Pontianak. However, the Borneo State never materialized, thanks mostly to the opposition of Dewan Banjar and the rejection by many of Borneo's Dewan of the possibility of Sultan Hamid

---

105 Schiller, *The Formation*, p. 188. The Federasi Kalimantan Tenggara originally consisted of the Pulau Laut, Pegatan, and Cantung Sampanahan Autonomous Regions.

106 Interviews with Tajib Kasuma, former member of Dewan Kutai, June 14, 1979; and Pangeran Mohammad Noor, Jakarta, November 25, 1977.

107 For a discussion of how the Republicans used the Federal scheme to enhance their cause, see George McT. Kahin, *Nationalism and Revolution in Indonesia* (Ithaca: Cornell University Press, 1952), pp. 351-90. The Republican faction in NIT's Parliament was led by Arnold Mononutu. In its final days, NIT was governed by a Republican cabinet under the Premiership of Ir. Putuhena. See *Republik Indonesia: Propinsi Sulawesi* (Jakarta: Kementerian Penerangan RI, 1953), pp. 171-75. In South Kalimantan, the Republicans had established a political party, Serikat Kerakjatan Indonesia (SKI), that had close relations with the guerrillas. When the Dutch insisted on establishing the Dewan Banjar, SKI sent a delegation to meet Vice President Hatta in Yogyakarta. Hatta agreed with the condition that SKI, and the Republicans, had to dominate the Dewan Banjar, which they did. See Mugnie Djunaidi, "Peranan Serikat Kerakyatan Indonesia (S.K.I.) Dalam Perjuangan Menegakkan Kemerdekaan Indonesiadi Kalimantan Selatan" (MA thesis, IKIP Malang, 1975), pp. 101-8.

Algadrie II of Pontianak being appointed as the *Walinegara*.[108]

Because of pro-Republican sentiments among the Kutai aristocrats, especially the middle-level aristocrats, the Samarinda Republicans formed a working relationship with them at East Borneo's Dewan. However, the Samarinda Republicans were angered by the Dutch policy of abolishing the prewar special status of Samarinda. Instead of being governed directly by the Dutch, Samarinda was put under the sultanate's administration. This policy led to the emergence of an anti-*swapraja* movement among the Samarinda Republicans in the early 1950s. The Dutch policy of appeasement towards the Kutai aristocrats also included the appointment of a Resident for East Borneo in Samarinda, and the appointment of Sultan Kutai's half brother, Aji Pangeran Kertanegara, who was a member of the *Kerapatan* (Kutai's cabinet), as a minister of state in the BFO (Bijeenkomstvoor Federal Overleg, Federal Consultative Assembly) cabinet in Jakarta.[109]

But from 1948 onward the Kutai aristocrats were quite different from prewar Kutai. Young aristocrats with Republican sympathies, such as Afloes and Kariowiti, had important positions that enabled them to help the Republican cause. Jealousy within the immediate family of the Sultan had led some of them to forge ties with the Republic, especially after the appointment of Kertanegara as minister. His half-brother, Aji Pangeran Temenggung Pranoto, was the police chief of Kutai, and in his official capacity had turned a blind eye to *lasykar* activities within his territory.[110]

---

108   In addition to the traditional rivalry between the various Sultans, many members of the Dewan Banjar and Dewan Kalimantan Timur disliked the idea of having Sultan Hamid II as *Walinegara*. He was considered very pro-Dutch, having achieved the rank of Lieutenant Colonel in the KL (Dutch Royal Army). Sultan Hamid's candidacy was backed by West Borneo's Dayak leader, J.C. Oevang Oeray (interview with AR Djokoprawiro, July 7, 1979). East Borneo wanted to have Parikesit as *Walinegara* since his apolitical nature would allow the daily government functions to fall into the hands of pro-Republican administrators. The opposition of Dewan Banjar to the Borneo State proposition was a crucial one, because the Dutch had planned to place the Borneo State's capital in Banjarmasin. Moreover, the guerrillas of Hassan Basri gave additional strength to the Republicans in Dewan Banjar. See Djunaidi, "Peranan," p. 111. See also, ***Rentjana Garis Besar Negara Kesatuan Kalimantan*** (Banjarmasin: Panitia Perantjang Negara Federasi Borneo Kalimantan, November 1948), p. 10.

109   Aji Pangeran Kertanegara was appointed by Van Mook as Secretary of State for Affairs of the Self-Governing Lands (Menteri Negara Urusan Swapraja) in the so-called "Interim Federal Government" of Indonesia in March 1948. See Schiller, *The Formation*, pp. 45-46.

110   Interviews with Aji Raden Djokoprawiro, Malang, July 7, 1979, and Tayib Kasuma, Tenggarong, June 19, 1979.

Given the uncertainty of the outcome of the conflict between the Dutch and the Indonesian Republicans, Kutai aristocrats were in the position of playing both sides of the street. As a result, they ruled differently and afforded better treatment to Kutai's population than in the prewar period. Moreover, the existence of Dewan at the *swapraja* levels had given the population considerable leverage over the Sultans. The leadership of the Dewan had mostly fallen into the hands of pro-Republican aristocrats, such as Afloes and Kariowiti in Kutai.[111]

In joining the Dewan, the Samarinda Republicans were in a difficult position. On the one hand, they still resented the Kutai sultanate and had formed an anti-*swapraja* movement. On the other hand, the Samarinda Republicans were accused by the Balikpapan *pejuang* of having cooperated with the Dutch-created Dewan. The feeling was especially bitter because Samarinda Republicans had taken over the leadership of INI, an organization known to have been established by the Balikpapan *pejuang*. Moreover, Samarinda Republicans, working together as a cohesive group, had been able to use INI as their own political vehicle, much to the disadvantage of the Balikpapan *pejuang* who were quite divided on the Dewan participation issue. Hence, the differences between Samarinda and Balikpapan were further widened by their different experiences during the Revolutionary period and their different tactical responses to the conditions they faced.

Soon after the agreed upon termination of the conflict at the KMB (Round Table Conference) discussions at The Hague in 1949, the Samarinda Republicans made close contact with some Kutai aristocrats who had pro-Republican leanings. It was hoped that these contacts would speed up the transfer of East Borneo from RUSI (Republican Union of States of Indonesia) to the unitary state.[112] Indeed, East Borneo was effectively incorporated into the unitary state in April 1950, four months before the formal incorporation ceremony of August 1950. The ceremony took place in Samarinda. At it, Afloes, then the Acting Resident of the

---

111 In the Dewan Kutai, for example, leadership was exercised by INI leaders, such as Abdul Azis Samad, while in Bulungan, it was exercised by Rasjid Sutan Radja Emas. For a brief biography of Rasjid Sutan Radja Emas, see Biographical Appendix and **Buku MPR 1971**, p. 983.

112 The INI Samarinda had its representative observing the Round Table Conference in The Hague, Inche Abdul Muis, who was also a member of Dewan Kalimantan Timur. This led to the accusation by Balikpapan *pejuang* that the INI were "cooperating" with the Dutch.

RUSI for East Borneo, handed over his authority to Dr. Murdjani, who had just been appointed Indonesian governor of Kalimantan by the Central Government.[113] Afloes was soon to be replaced by Roeslan Muljohardjo as the first Republican-appointed Resident of the East Kalimantan Residency in Samarinda. Hence, East Kalimantan was to be incorporated into the Indonesian administration as well.

While the civil administration was having its own change of guard in Samarinda, there had been two other important developments in the region. The first was the creation of military headquarters for East Borneo in Balikpapan, institutionalizing the differences between these two cities. Various *lasykar* were merged into one battalion of the TNI (Tentara Nasional Indonesia, Indonesian National Army), and they took over the security of Balikpapan, Samarinda, and other towns from the KNIL. Most of these *lasykar* saw Balikpapan as their capital and, although some were residing in Samarinda, they formed a close political alliance with Balikpapan. By December 1951, separate battalions were already stationed in Balikpapan, Tarakan, and Samarinda under the command of Regiment 22 of TT (Tentara dan Territorium, Army and Territorial Command) VI Kalimantan. The first commander of Regiment 22 was Major Sentot Iskandardinata, who was succeeded in 1955 by Major Ibnu Subroto, and in 1957, by Lieutenant Colonel R. Hartojo.[114]

The choice of Balikpapan as the headquarters of the military establishment for East Kalimantan had placed this city in a new position in its competition with Samarinda. In Balikpapan, the army officers were getting along well with the *pejuang*, most of whom had recently left the army. Their guerrilla experiences and armed struggle against the Dutch, even if only in the form of mass demonstrations, had given these two groups a common feeling of solidarity although they had fought in different places. Their close relationship was to be institutionalized later on in the Angkatan 45 (1945 generation), a veterans' organization under the domination of Balikpapan *pejuang* and the supervision of the military commander.

---

113 Dr. Mas Moerdjani was replaced by Resident Sutan Kumala Pontas, and later on, by Governor Milono. Moerdjani's appointment as the first Governor after 1950 had created an uproar among the Banjarese Republicans who demanded the return of their fellow Banjarese, Ir. Pangeran Mohammad Noor. Interview with Mrs. Soeminie Moerdjani, Jakarta, August 16, 1979.

114 See *Sejarah Kodam Mulawarman*, p. 24.

The second development was related to the decline of the aristocracy's economic resources resulting from the transfer of the oil royalties to the hands of the Central Government. Oil royalties were to be negotiated directly between the oil companies and the Central Government departments. The region, thus, would no longer get its share of royalties directly from the oil companies, but through subsidies from the Central Government, allocated in the annual provincial budget. These subsidies were given directly to the provincial government in Banjarmasin, from which the East Kalimantan residency would get its own share together with the other residencies. This policy resulted in a loss of royalties for East Kalimantan, since the provincial budget was always biased in favor of Banjarmasin and the South Kalimantan residency, where the Governor resided.[115]

The biggest loser under this arrangement, nevertheless, was the aristocracy of East Kalimantan. The immediate families of the Sultans suffered the most because they suddenly found themselves in the position of economic pariahs. At the end of the nineteenth century, the Dutch had banned any company owned by the Sultans. Hence, the sultanates were entirely dependent on Dutch royalties and favors. As a result, many of the companies established by Sultan Sulaiman in Kutai were taken over by the Dutch in order to deprive the sultanate of any economic resources of its own.[116]

Having felt satisfied with the royalties provided by the Dutch, the Sultan never foresaw the possibility that royalty payments would end. Of course, even if he had foreseen these changes, Sultan Parikesit would not have been able to hedge against them. He was not an industrious man willing to undertake business ventures as his grandfather had been. In sum, because of his dependency on the Dutch oil royalties, he not only lost his only significant source of revenue, but also lost control over a

---

115 The appointment of a non-Banjarese as Governor was partly aimed at easing the apprehensions of the other regions regarding the fairness of the budget distributions. However, since the South Kalimantan residency was the biggest in terms of population, it was allocated most of the budget. This led to demands for the creation of separate provinces from the other regions of Kalimantan. See, for example, **Harian Indonesia Merdeka** (Banjarmasin) January 8, 1951, on the demands of the political parties from West Kalimantan for their own province on the basis that "[they] could not make progress as long as the capital was in Banjarmasin."

116 For a description of the economic activities of Sultan Sulaiman, see Djokoprawiro et al., "Sejarah," pp. 49-53.

once economically dependent aristocracy that now was forced to look out financially for itself.

The only avenue open to the aristocracy was to seek appointments as *pegawai daerah* (provincial civil servants) in the Kutai *swapraja* which continued to exist up to 1957. However, since the provincial bureaucracy in Banjarmasin and the Resident's office in Samarinda were controlled by the Republicans, loyalty to the Republican cause during the Revolution had become an important qualification for an appointment. Moreover, since most aristocrats had paid little attention to educational achievement in the prewar period, only a few who had graduated from OSVIA could be appointed to the really important bureaucratic positions.

Under these circumstances the middle-level aristocrats, who in the prewar period had not been much involved in the extravagant life style of the Kutai sultanate but had pursued governmental careers, were able to rise politically. It was from this stratum that leaders such as Afloes, Kariowiti, Aji Raden Sajid Mohammad, Aji Raden Usman, Aji Raden Padmo, and Sayid Mochsen came. They were to play prominent roles in East Kalimantan politics in the 1950s and 1960s.

Among the immediate family of Sultan Parikesit, only his half-brother, Pranoto, was to survive the crisis. Having shown sympathy for the Republican cause in the Revolutionary period, Pranoto was able to climb the bureaucratic ladder, so that by 1956 he was appointed Resident of East Kalimantan. He was helped by his fellow Kutai aristocrat, Aji Raden Djokoprawiro, who had gone to Jakarta to become a member of Parliament, representing the PIR-Hazairin.[117]

The aristocracies of Bulungan, Pasir, Gunung Tabur, and Sambaliung fared better than the Kutai aristocracy. Although they were put aside into the marginal *swapraja*-level leadership positions, they were not much resented by the Republicans. Some even survived up to the 1970s, although the Bulungan aristocracy was to be destroyed in 1964 by the then regional military commander (Panglima Daerah Militer Pangdam)

---

117 Aside from promoting Pranoto, Djokoprawiro was also instrumental in persuading the new Governor of Kalimantan in 1956, fellow PIR member, R.T.A. Milono, to appoint fellow Kutai aristocrat, A.R. Afloes, as Resident of West Kalimantan. In promoting *pamong praja* members of PIR, Djokoprawiro was helped by the former minister of interior and PIR chairman, Dr. Hazairin, and the former secretary general of the Ministry of Interior, Djanoeismadi, who was also deputy chairman of the PIR Central Board. Interview with Djokoprawiro, July 7, 1979.

of East Kalimantan, Brigadier General Soeharjo.[118]

Despite their decline, the aristocracy were able to adjust to the politics of the early 1950s. The expansion of political parties to provinces outside Java during these years was the most important single event that helped the aristocrats. Since the national political parties were running against time to prepare themselves for the oncoming elections, they embraced the pre-existing factions and organizations which had existed at the regional level. While preference was generally given to groups and organizations with compatible ideologies and political beliefs, ideological differences were often put aside in favor of forging coalitions that might produce an electoral victory. This policy, above all, resulted in the accommodation of an ideologically diverse regional leadership into the national political party system. Consequently, the various local leaders in East Borneo became the leaders of national parties in their respective regions. There were, nonetheless, some regional and local leaders who preferred to run their own political organization and rejected any formal ties with the national parties.

Political developments in East Kalimantan in early 1950 exemplify this regional political trend. Already by then the INI branches of Tarakan and Samarinda had proclaimed themselves to be regional branches of the Indonesian National Party (PNI). The INI chairman, Abdul Muis Hassan, was appointed as a member of the PNI Central Board, whereas the chairman of INI Tarakan, Rasjid Sutan Radja Emas, was appointed as PNI representative in the provisional Parliament.[119] Most of the *pejuang* of Balikpapan and Samarinda, on the other hand, joined the Murba party on an individual basis while a few entered the Indonesian Socialist Party (PSI). Hence, they did not join a single party *en bloc* as the INI of Samarinda and Tarakan had done.[120] The *pejuang* joined Murba and PSI

---

118 Brigadier General Soeharjo did not totally destroy the Berau aristocracy. In fact, the Pranoto-appointed Bupati, former Head of Autonomous Region, Aji Raden Mohammad Ajub, was to govern his *kabupaten* until 1964, due mostly to his ability to become the leader of the NU at the provincial level. For a brief biography of A.R.M. Ajub, see Biographical Appendix and **Buku MPR, 1971,** p. 764.

119 It should be noted that since 1950, Rasjid has lived in Jakarta whereas I. A. Muis stayed in Samarinda until 1960. For a brief biography of A. M. Hassan, see Dr. O. G. Roeder, **Who's Who in Indonesia** (Jakarta: Gunung Agung, 1970), pp. 502-3.

120 Husein Jusuf, Djunaid Sanusie, and Mohammad Sabrie joined the Murba party while Siebold Mewengkang joined the Partai Buruh. Oemar Dachlan joined the PSI, while Aminuddin Nata

apparently for religious reasons. Moreover, it was difficult to find followers of the Indonesian Communist Party (PKI) among the Islamic-oriented Banjarese in Balikpapan and Samarinda. Beyond this, the Balikpapan and Samarinda *pejuang* had contacts mostly with the *pejuang* in the Murba and PSI in Jakarta.

Similarly, the Kutai aristocracy mostly gave its support to two different national political parties. Pranoto and many others gave regional support to Djokoprawiro in Jakarta, becoming leaders of the East Kalimantan branch of the Greater Indonesia Party (PIR). Another faction, led by Afloes and Kariowiti, helped to provide a bridge between the Kutai and the Banjarese by becoming leaders of Masjumi. Sultan Parikesit, however, took no part, and had no interest, in political life. His half-brother, Kertanegara, also took no part in politics. He was disqualified from pursuing a political career since he had been appointed as a BFO (the Dutch-sponsored Federalist effort) minister. With the partisan division of the aristocracy, internal rivalry within the Kutai aristocracy was subsumed into the existing political party system.[121]

It should be noted, however, that the Bulungan and Berau aristocracies were not as fortunate as other aristocratic groups. Resenting the Tarakan-based Republicans, the Bulungan aristocracy had divorced itself from the national political scene and developed its own informal organization, led by its own leaders. While they commanded a certain strength within the Tanjungselor-Tanjung Palas complex, the Bulungan aristocrats had lost their political authority in Tarakan and the interior, where Christian missionaries had significantly influenced the Kenyah-Kayan Dayaks. The Berau aristocracy, likewise, was too small and insignificant to play a role in provincial politics. A similar fate overtook the Pasir aristocracy, which came to be governed by the Banjarese. Hence, among the East Kalimantan aristocracies, only the Pranoto faction and Afloes group were able to adjust successfully to the new power structure and new political

---

refrained from joining any political party although he was quite sympathetic to the PSI. Fachrul Baraqbah was the leader of the PKI in East Kalimantan. All of them were *pejuang* during the Revolutionary period.

121 The real loser was Aji Pangeran Sosronegoro, the fourth member of the Kutai cabinet. He was also a half-brother of Sultan Parikesit but had no strong educational background. He could not compete with A. P. Kertanegara in the late 1940s and was left behind by Pangeran Pranoto in the 1950s.

game rules. These aristocratic groups had been successful because they helped the national political parties expand into the region. Now, due to their efforts, they could compete with the Samarinda Republicans who led the PNI and the Balikpapan-Samarinda *pejuang* who were centered in the PSI and Murba.

Aside from the *pejuang's* parties, the Islamic parties were to play an important role in regional politics. Although they did not have important *pejuang* as their leaders, the Islamic parties benefited from the existence of informal *pengajian* (religious activity) organizations, the existence of the Nahdhatul Ulama (NU), and Muhammadiyah's importance to the Masjumi party. As a result of their performance in the 1955 election, in particular, the Islamic parties were able to play important roles in the local political process (see Table 4).

The 1955 election had a different impact on the three major political actors in East Kalimantan. The PNI victory at the provincial level resulted from the party's ability to forge a feeling of nationalism among the various ethnic groups. The Samarinda Republicans had been able to broaden their bases of power to the interior areas of Kutai, where the Dayak chiefs were quite happy to identify themselves with a non-Islamic party like PNI, the nationalist cause, and Sukarno's leadership. Moreover, PNI's dominant position among the *pamong praja* corps enabled them to penetrate the difficult regions of the interior, which most of the other parties had neglected.

The PNI's success brought its leaders into prominent positions in the PNI Central Board. While Sutan Radja Emas had already moved to Jakarta, Abdul Muis Hassan and Inche Abdul Muis were soon to follow him and to become known in the Jakarta political arena. Hence, they advanced from being mere provincial politicians into being national politicians. This national status alone differentiated them from their immediate rivals, the leaders of NU and Masjumi, who were mostly local *ulama* and leaders of the Banjarese community, without ties to national politics.

Following its electoral success, the PNI scored its first parliamentary victory with the passage of a law mandating that by the beginning of 1957 East Kalimantan was to become a province of its own. Ever since the beginning of 1950, the PNI had resented the reestablishment of a *swapraja* in East Kalimantan. They particularly resented the continuation of the late 1940s Dutch policy which had put Samarinda under the administration of Kutai. By early 1950, they had been able to persuade Republican Resident, Roeslan Muljohardjo, to move the Kutai *swapraja* from Tenggarong to Samarinda. This move in effect loosened the Sultan's grip over Samarinda's daily affairs. Though Sultan Parikesit was still the head of the *swapraja*, he did not want to travel to Samarinda to take care of governmental affairs. Daily tasks then fell into the hands of the DPD (Dewan Pemerintah Daerah -- Regional Government Council) which was headed by a Samarinda-PNI man, Abdul Azis Samad.[122] Despite its *de facto* power over the Kutai *swapraja*, the PNI still demanded the abolition of the *swapraja* office as part of its national policy of democratizing the political process.[123] East Kalimantan's PNI leaders also disliked the fact that Banjarmasin dominated the provincial bureaucracy of Kalimantan at the expense of other regions.

The East Kalimantan *pejuang*, on the other hand, did not fare well in the election of 1955. The main party representing the *pejuang*, Murba, was even defeated by the Catholic party. Murba's support came mostly from the Balikpapan region where almost all the *pejuang* chose to join that party. In Samarinda, *pejuang* support was so divided among the PSI, Murba, PSII, and even the PKI that the *pejuang* could not compete against the more unified Banjarese support for the PNI and Islamic parties, NU, and Masjumi. Indeed, among the *pejuang*-supported parties, only the PSI was able to get enough votes to gain a position for itself in the Big Four. The PSI had also gained considerable influence within the provincial bureaucracy, due in no small part to the work of the PSI Resident, Achmad Arief gelar Datuk Majoe Orang of Minangkabau origin.[124]

In contrast, in spite of its internal divisions, the aristocracy achieved quite a good election result. Under Pranoto's patronage, PIR had gained a fifth position in East Kalimantan, well above its national position.[125] Its

---

122 When Azis Samad came to head the provincial leadership, the DPD was headed by another Banjarese-PNI member, Mansjursjah. Interview with Azis Samad, June 20, 1979.

123 Interview with Abdul Muis Hassan, Jakarta, July 12, 1979.

124 For a brief biography of Achmad Arief Datoek Madjoe Orang, see Biographical Appendix, **Daftar Tjalon-tjalon Konstituante 1955** (Jakarta: Kementerian Penerangan R.I., 1955), p. 188, and Oemar Dachlan, "Perkembangan Pemerintahan Kalimantan Timur" (Samarinda: 1967, typescript), p. 6.

125 At the national level, PIR-Hazairin received only 0.3 percent of the votes and was in the 22nd position among the contestants, with only one DPR seat. Hence, Djokoprawiro failed in his

bases of support were mostly in the bureaucratic structure where Kutai aristocrats had tried to regain political power. As the Minister of the Interior in 1954, Hazairin had been able to advance many Kutai aristocrats within the bureaucracy, such that by 1956 Pranoto was appointed as East Kalimantan Resident because of his seniority within the *pamong praja's* ranks.

Hence, by the end of the election in 1955, the Balikpapan *pejuang* held the worst political position among the three major political actors. Not only were they still under the rule of the Kutai *swapraja*, which placed their interests behind the interests both of the aristocrats and of the Samarinda PNI leadership, but they had been unable to achieve any electoral success. Having been denied access to the bureaucratic structure (due mostly to their inadequate educational qualifications) and lacking a mass following, they could not possibly hope to win any future elections. They could only hope to obtain political opportunities for themselves by exploiting their personal contacts, both with fellow *pejuang* among the military officers at Balikpapan and with national leaders. Contacts within the Angkatan 45 organization, in particular, opened up political doors for them. It was through this organization that the leader of the Balikpapan *pejuang*, Husein Jusuf, was appointed a member of the Dewan Perancang Nasional (National Planning Body) in the late 1950s.[126]

By the end of 1956, then, East Kalimantan was ripe for further political competition between these three important groups. The appointment of Pranoto as the first Governor of East Kalimantan in 1958 gave his faction of Kutai aristocrats a leading advantage in provincial politics. He appointed his fellow aristocrat and PIR member, Aji Raden Padmo, as the first Bupati of Kutai while in other *kabupaten* he also advanced the career of fellow aristocrats.[127] However, his position was to be challenged by both the Samarinda-based PNI leadership and the Balikpapan *pejuang*.

---

attempt to bring other Kutai aristocrats into national politics. For the national results, see A. van Marle, "The First Indonesian Parliamentary Elections," *Indonesië*, 9 (1956) [The Hague]: 258.

126 For a brief biography of Husein Jusuf, see Biographical Appendix.

127 For a brief biography of AR Padmo, see Biographical Appendix and **Buku MPR 1971**, p. 763. Aside from AR Padmo, Pranoto also appointed fellow aristocrats, A.R.S. Mohammad as Mayor of Balikpapan; A.R.M. Ajub as Bupati of Berau; Andi Tjatjo gelar Datu Mihardja as Bupati of Bulungan, while the Bupatiship of Pasir went to a Sundanese *pamong praja*, Yudabrata. Only the position of Mayor of Samarinda was in military hands, Captain Sudjono AJ was the Mayor of Samarinda.

Table 4. The results of the 1955 election by *kabupaten* and party

Party/Organization	Kutai[a]	Berau	Bulungan[b]	Total
PNI[c]	6,231	1,136	15,700	45,100
Masjumi[d]	4,994	2,168	7,185	44,347
NU[e]	16,431	3,444	920	20,795
PSI[f]	11,865	288	876	13,029
PIR (Hazairin)[g]	8,933	3	335	9,271
PKI[h]	6,718	788	703	8,209
PSII[i]	7,018	75	308	7,401
Katolik[j]	3,948	6	199	4,153
Murba[k]	2,389	880	698	3,967
Andi Tjatjo gelar Datu Wihardja dkk[l]	61	3	3,811	3,875
Partai Rakjat Indonesia[m]	2,646	1	46	2,693
Parkindo[n]	1,440	75	1,113	2,585
PPPRI[o]	1,332	880	698	1,708
Gerakan Pembela Pantjasila[p]	587	10	1,167	1,764
Partai Buruh[q]	1,064	35	257	1,356
PPTI[r]	1,129	30	83	1,242
PRN[s]	696	55	74	825
Parindra[t]	574	16	42	632
Mutung gelar Mas Perwiro[u]	40	635	26	701
Baperki[v]	293	106	137	536
Gerakan Banteng RI[w]	112	4	19	135
Partai Persatuan Daya (k)[x]	-	-	-	-

Sources: Alfian, **Hasil Pemilihan Umum 1955 untuk DPR** (Jakarta: Lednud, 1971), pp. 137-41; Tjilik Riwut, **Kalimantan Membangun** (Jakarta: P.T. Jayakarta Agung, 1979), p. 193; Herbert Feith, *The Indonesian Election of 1955* (Ithaca: Cornell Modern Indonesia Project, 1957), p. 70.

[a] In the 1955 election, the *kabupaten* of Kutai still administered the present-day *kotamadya* of Balikpapan and Samarinda. Hence, the strength of each contestant should be seen in light of this administrative division.

[b] Bulungan *kabupaten* also included the Tarakan *kecamatan* where about a fifth of the voters lived.

[c] The candidates from the PNI for DPR were mostly Samarinda leaders, led by Abdul Muis Hassan, Anang Suleiman, I. A. Muis and Rasjid Sutan Radja Emas. The only candidate from Balikpapan was a Javanese, Mas Tjokrosumarto. See **Daftar Tjalon-tjalon DPR 1955** (Jakarta: Kementerian Penerangan R.I., 1955), p. 163.

[d] The leading candidate was a Banjarese of Samarinda, Ahmad Jusuf, who was a leader of the Muhammadiyah, and AR Kariowiti, who was then the Wedana of Balikpapan. AR Afloes was running as a lesser candidate for the South Kalimantan electorate. Ibid., p. 164.

[e] The candidates of NU were mostly Samarinda Banjarese; none of them were known provincially. The only aristocrat was Sayid Gasjim bin Sayid Idrus Baraqbah, the elder brother of Fachrul Baraqbah. Ibid., p. 164.

[f] The candidate from PSI was Abdul Gani, a Banjarese *pamong praja*.

[g] The list of PIR candidates was led by AR Padmo, to be followed by Tajib Kasuma and a Kutai-Melayu *pamong praja*, Encik Abdurrachim gelar Encik Mas Natadjaja. Ibid., p. 166.

[h] Fahrul Baraqbah who was from a Kutai Arabic aristocratic background was the leading candidate of the PKI. Ibid., p. 166.

[i] The candidates were mostly Balikpapan Banjarese who were not grouped into a strong party.

[j] At that time, the Catholic Party still did not have a local leadership of Dayak origins.

[k] The candidates from Murba were led by Husein Jusuf, followed by Anang Atjil and Djunaid Sanusie; all of them were *pejuang* from Balikpapan and Samarinda. Ibid., p. 163.

[l] Andi Tjatjo led a local slate from the Bulungan aristocracy which had won the local DPRD. It consisted of Andi Tjatjo (later to become Bupati of Bulungan in 1960), Datu Badaruddin bin Datu Mahkota of the Bulungan sultanate and Achmad Daud Daeng Panggiling. It was a Moslem-based group of Bulungan and Buginese people. Ibid., p. 165.

[m] The PRI only represented the Javanese in Balikpapan who did not have many ties to the local groups. Ibid., p. 164.

[n] The only local leader from Parkindo was a Minahasan *pamong praja*, Damus Maneng Frans, who was a Wedana at Tarakan, and in 1959 became the first Bupati of Berau. Ibid., p. 164.

[o] The vote for the PPPRI mostly came from its police members and families. Since many NCOs were Banjarese, the PPPRI benefited from this fact. Ibid., p. 159.

[p] The slate of the GPPS was led by A. P. Sosronegoro. The only local aristocrat who followed him was of Melayu origin, Encik Muhammad Sjaradin. Ibid., p. 165.

[q] The only candidate of the Partai Buruh was Siebold Mewengkang. Ibid.,

[r] The PPTI had a small following among the Islamic Banjarese of Samarinda who provided its only candidate. Ibid.

[s] The PRN did not have a prominent candidate from East Kalimantan. On its South Kalimantan slate, it included AP Kertanegara, who was then residing in Surabaya. His absence from the East Kalimantan slate was possibly caused by the fact that he could have been defeated there because of his cooperation with the Dutch.

[t] Parindra's slate was led by its prewar leader, Bustani HS from Samarinda. Ibid., p. 163.

[u] Mutung gelar Mas Perwiro was another local leader from Gunung Tabur who was in competition with A.R.M. Ajub, who had his own slate.

[v] Despite a sizable number of Chinese, Baperki did not get many votes, possibly because most Chinese were aliens.

[w] It was a Samarinda-based organization of *pejuang*, led by Herman Runturambi and RM Hidajat. It was considered to be close to the Murba party.

[x] Despite its name, the party was mostly West Borneo-based. Its support came from the Land Dayaks, and it did not have many followers in Central and East Kalimantan. It was led by two leaders, F.C. Palaunsuka and J. C. Oevang Oeray. Palaunsuka later joined the Catholic Party and when it was incorporated into the PDI, he served as member of the Central Board. In 1987, he was elected as a member of the DPR from PDI representing West Kalimantan province. Oevang Oeray was later appointed as Governor of West Kalimantan during the period of Guided Democracy. In early 1970 he joined Golkar and was a member of its DPR faction until his death in 1987.

By 1959, the PNI had taken advantage of Law Number 1/1957 on local government, under which the Governor had to work together with the Kepala Daerah (Regional Head).[128] Since the PNI controlled the provincial DPRD, they elected their own leader, Inche Abdul Muis, as the Kepala Daerah.[129] With the increasing power of the PNI in national politics, its regional leaders were able to persuade Sukarno to appoint Abdul Muis Hassan as the new Governor of East Kalimantan in 1962, a position which combined the offices previously held by Pranoto and Inche Abdul Muis.[130]

It was under Abdul Muis Hassan that the PNI started to dominate the bureaucratic structure at the provincial and *kabupaten* levels to such a degree that by the end of his governorship in 1966, Muis Hassan had been able to build a PNI-controlled *pamong praja* in East Kalimantan.[131] During

---

128 For a discussion of UU Number 1/1957, see for example, J. Wajong, **Azas dan Tujuan Pemerintahan Daerah** (Jakarta: Jambatan, 1975), pp. 46-64. In other provinces, the PNI had been able to put in its men as Regional Heads. For example, it had succeeded in making Hadisubeno the Regional Head of Central Java and Kosasih the Regional Head of West Java. However, its attempt to place Dul Arnowo as Regional Head in East Java was blocked by a persistent *pamong praja*-minded Governor, Samadikoen.

129 It seems that the Samarinda Banjarese had been able to take advantage of I. A. Muis's short tenure as Governor. Although a prominent leader of the PNI, I. A. Muis was not that popular among the Banjarese who preferred their own man, Abdul Muis Hassan.

130 This was made possible by Penpres (Presidential Decree) number 6/1959. By 1962 when Abdul Muis Hassan was appointed Governor, he had been a member of Parliament and was well known in Jakarta politics. Moreover, the military could no longer resist the temptation to replace Pranoto, who was considered the leading figure of the Kutai aristocracy.

131 About 75 percent of the *camat* were PNI men, according to the leader of the PNI at that time. Interview with Anang Sulaiman, Samarinda, June 18, 1979.

his governorship, Muis Hassan minimized PSI and PIR control over the bureaucracy by giving unimportant jobs to their members. Moreover, he created young cadres of PNI-oriented *pamong praja* by sending young members of the PNI to universities in Java. The majority of these cadres were Banjarese, but there were also a few Kutai within this group.[132]

The creation of East Kalimantan province also had important repercussions for the Balikpapan *pejuang*. The Balikpapan *pejuang* were again able to challenge the Kutai aristocracy by allying themselves with the military hierarchy of Kodam (Regional Military Command) Mulawarman, which had been established in July 1958, following the creation of East Kalimantan province. The Kodam Mulawarman was to have territorial responsibility over East Kalimantan, concurrently with the provincial civilian administration. This territorial arrangement gave rise to a dual leadership in provincial politics. Balikpapan was to become the military capital of East Kalimantan, and with the establishment of the provincial branches of the national departments, Balikpapan became the site of many government offices as well.[133] Because of its communications, and especially airport, facilities, Balikpapan was chosen over Samarinda as the site for regional government offices. The important office of the Governor, however, remained located in Samarinda. Balikpapan's *pejuang* made use of Balikpapan's new-found administrative importance not only to destroy gradually their traditional arch-rivals, the Kutai aristocracy, but also to take over provincial power from their fellow Republican rivals in Samarinda.

---

132 Among these young university graduates Djakfar Achmad, Mohammad Ardans, and Achmad Dahlan were PNI cadres. In the mid-1960s, they started their careers in important positions at the Governor's office as bureau chiefs. Achmad Dahlan was appointed as Bupati of Kutai in 1965 and M. Ardans as Governor in 1988.

133 The offices of the representatives of the various government departments were located in Balikpapan, including the Kejaksaan Tinggi (Provincial Prosecutor's office), the Police Chief's office, the *Kepala Pos* (Post Office), provincial head office, and most of the State Bank's headquarters.

CHAPTER FIVE
PEJUANG IN POWER AND THE COLLAPSE OF THE ARISTOCRACY

By early 1960, Kodam Mulawarman was led by a young *pejuang* officer, Lieutenant Colonel R. Soeharjo. He was the Chief of Staff of the first Regional Military Commander (Pangdam), Colonel Hartojo, and was promoted to the Panglimaship when Hartojo left for Jakarta. The appointment of Soeharjo had a profound effect on the rise of the *pejuang* in the early 1960s in East Kalimantan politics. A Javanese *priyayi* like Hartojo, Soeharjo did not share the cautious and restrained mood of the former. With his strong revolutionary spirit, Soeharjo was welcomed by the Balikpapan *pejuang* who saw in him the leader they had long waited for.[134]

There were two important groups which had been looking for leadership. The first was the Balikpapan-Samarinda *pejuang* who resented both the leadership of Governor Pranoto and the rise of the Samarinda-based PNI. The second group was made up mostly of Javanese oil workers in Balikpapan, who were increasingly under the leadership of the PKI-affiliated union, Perbum (Persatuan Buruh Minyak -- Association of Oil Workers). Soeharjo soon developed a close relationship with these two groups, and this put him in the forefront of Balikpapan's leadership to the detriment of the PNI-leaning, Samarinda-based Banjarese.

The appointment of Muis Hassan as the new Governor in 1962 and his stress on the PNI-zation of the provincial bureaucracy had increased

---

134 Soeharjo not only had fought during the Revolution for the Indonesian revolutionary forces, but had served as a military aide to the visiting leader of the Democratic Republic of Vietnam, Ho Chi Minh. (Interview with General Nasution, Jakarta, July 14, 1979.) For a brief biography of Soeharjo, see Biographical Appendix and *Sejarah Kodam Mulawarman*, p. 24.

political competition in East Kalimantan. By that time, military officers were increasingly drawn into civilian jobs under the famous "middle way" and "army dual function" philosophy of General Nasution. Soeharjo used this philosophy to further the interest of the army by proposing army officers for Bupatiships, steering into direct conflict with Governor Muis Hassan. He was able to press for the appointment of his fellow Brawijaya officer, Captain Sudjono AJ, as the Mayor of Samarinda, and then, another officer, Lieutenant Colonel Yatmo, as Bupati of Pasir.[135]

However, the main vehicle Soeharjo used to strengthen his position was the chairmanship of the Front Nasional, an institution created by President Sukarno as part of his Guided Democracy structure.[136] The East Kalimantan branch of the Front Nasional was created by a Presidential decree on April 15, 1961, and its membership was dominated by the *pejuang*.[137]

Aside from Soeharjo, the Provincial Board of the Front Nasional included Samarinda *pejuang*, Harun Nafsi and Sayid Fachrul Baraqbah. The former represented the Angkatan 45 while the latter represented the PKI. The leader of Perbum in Balikpapan, M. Turangan, was a member of the daily board, while the secretariat was headed by Soeharjo's fellow officer, Major Roesmono. A provincial leader of the PKI-affiliated women's organization, Gerwani, Mrs. Soetedjo, was appointed as deputy secretary. The only leader of the Samarinda-based Banjarese PNI, Asmuransjah, became its deputy chairman.

By including the PKI in the leadership of the Front Nasional, Soeharjo gained a strong constituency among the oil workers in Tarakan and Balikpapan who had been under strong Perbum influence. In his capacity as Pangdam, Soeharjo increased the influence of Perbum by arresting Mewengkang, the leader of its rival labor organization, on the basis of vague allegations. Mewengkang was to become the first victim

---

135 Captain Sudjono AJ was to be replaced by Soeharjo's man, Lieutenant Colonel Ngoedijo, in 1961. Lieutenant Colonel Sujatmo replaced a *pamong praja* Bupati, Zamzam.

136 The Front Nasional scheme was used to include the PKI in positions of national and local leadership which had been otherwise denied to them. For a discussion of the period of Guided Democracy, see Herbert Feith, "Dynamics of Guided Democracy," in *Indonesia*, ed. Ruth McVey (New Haven: HRAF, 1963), pp. 309-409.

137 For the list of membership see *Almanak Lembaga Negara dan Kepartaian* (Jakarta: Departemen Penerangan, 1961), pp. 412-13.

of Soeharjo's efforts to consolidate his power. He was released only after Soeharjo was replaced by Brigadier General Sumitro in March 1965.[138]

Within the provincial leadership of the PKI, Soeharjo found a willing ally in the person of Fachrul Baraqbah.[139] Fachrul was believed to be disappointed with the non-*pejuang* domination of the provincial leadership, although in 1960 he had been elected as one of the deputy chairmen of the DPRD. His closest associate was the leader of Perbum, Martono. Both men were close associates of Soeharjo.

In establishing the office of the provincial Front Nasional in Balikpapan, Soeharjo had also undermined the power of the Governor in Samarinda by appointing his own protégé, Lieutenant Colonel Sudjono, as Commander of Samarinda's Military District (Kodim). Hence, Fachrul and Harun Nafsi were to become the Front Nasional's men in Samarinda and, together with the Kodim, would become the center of anti-PNI forces in that capital.

Whereas Fachrul was a close associate of Colonel Soeharjo, his elder brother, Sayid Mochsen, was acting as a close adviser to Governor Muis Hassan. Hence, the two brothers were to become important actors in the politics of East Kalimantan and were the only Kutai aristocrats, albeit of Arabic origins, to do so.[140] Muis Hassan also worked closely with Abdul Azis Samad who was the Chairman of DPRD. In the Governor's office, young cadres of university-educated PNI members were starting to enter the bureaucracy, having just returned from Java. They were the children of Samarinda Banjarese who were given fellowships by the Yayasan Mulawarman, an education foundation jointly funded by the Kutai

---

138 Interview with Siebold Mewengkang, Balikpapan, June 28, 1979.
139 For a brief biography of Sayid Fachrul Baraqbah, see Biographical Appendix in this monograph.
140 The three brothers, Sayid Mochsen, Sayid Gasjim, and Fachrul Baraqbah were actually political leaders during the Guided Democracy period. Their prominence gave rise to some resentment among the Kutai aristocrats who considered them to be living extravagantly in exclusive surroundings. However, this resentment was probably more an outcome of the intense competition for bureaucratic and leadership posts that characterized this period. For a discussion of the resentment engendered by the Kutai "Arab" aristocrats' reluctance to let their daughters marry the Kutai aristocrats' sons, see Djokoprawiro, et al., "Sejarah," p. 37. See also, interview with AR Djokoprawiro, Malang, July 7, 1979. Such a feeling of resentment toward these three brothers was not prevalent among the members of other political groups, such as the PNI Banjarese or Islamic Banjarese, both of which had chosen these individuals of Arab descent as their leaders for the 1955 election.

swapraja and the provincial government. Their rise within the PNI-dominated provincial bureaucracy was quite fast, so that by 1965 some of them had been appointed as Bupati. Achmad Dahlan and Saleh Nafsi, for example, were appointed Bupati of Kutai and of Pasir, respectively. Another *sarjana* of PNI orientation, M. Ardans, was to rise within the provincial bureaucracy to become Sekwilda (provincial secretary) in 1979 and deputy governor in 1985. He was elected as Governor in 1988.[141] Some of the students who came from the lower levels of the Kutai aristocracy, the Awang, were embraced by the dominant PNI leaders.[142]

The Samarinda-based PNI also expanded its influence in accordance with the PNI's increasing power within the Guided Democracy structure in Jakarta. The PNI did not circumscribe its exercise of influence to the government bureaucracy. A branch of a PNI-affiliated university, Untag was established in Samarinda in 1963 and was later incorporated into the newly established state university, Universitas Mulawarman. The university served as a recruiting ground for young PNI cadres, broadening the bases of PNI support.

While attempting to expand its political power, the PNI had also begun to develop certain business activities. The most well-known was the shipping company PT Mahakam which provided regular service between Java and East Kalimantan. Since East Kalimantan was dependent on outside supplies for its daily consumption needs, a shipping company should have been a good business, especially with the backing of the PNI-dominated provincial bureaucracy. Inche Abdul Muis directed the company from Jakarta, and he used his Tokyo connections to get some ships from Japan. Up to 1965, the company was doing quite well, but poor management practices prevented it from becoming an important liner

---

141 Achmad Dahlan is the younger brother of a PSI *pejuang*, Oemar Dahlan, while Saleh Nafsi is the younger brother of another Samarinda *pejuang*, Harun Nafsi. Both of these young university graduates were considered to be close to the PNI, although later on they became prominent leaders of Golkar. In 1987, Achmad Dahlan became a member of the DPR in Jakarta representing Golkar until his death that year in a car accident. His wife was the daughter of prewar *pejuang*, A. M. Sangaji. The third university graduate, M. Ardans, married the daughter of a prominent bureaucrat of Kutai aristocratic origin, AR Padmo.

142 These students were the sons of PNI members. Awang Faisal and Awang Badaranie, for example, were the sons of PNI members Awang Ishak and Awang Abbas, respectively. In 1978, both Faisal and Badaranie were appointed Bupati, of Kutai and Pasir respectively.

service in the late 1960s and 1970s.[143] In fact, by the time of the timber harvesting boom in East Kalimantan in the late 1960s, PT Mahakam was in near bankruptcy and hence could not benefit from that boom. It was the Chinese-owned shipping companies of Surabaya that initially made profits from the transportation of timber from East Kalimantan in the late 1960s. But at that time, the exploitation of East Kalimantan timber was only partly underway, due mostly to the confusing array of regulations delineating the timber concession rights of the provincial government vis-à-vis the Directorate General of Forestry in Jakarta.

Despite Muis Hassan replacing Pranoto as Governor, the aristocracy managed to maintain its power in *kabupatan* Kutai. Aji Raden Padmo was still the Bupati, although various key positions in the Bupati's office had begun to be filled by Samarinda members of the PNI. Throughout East Kalimantan the PNI had largely gained power in the provincial bureaucracy mostly at the expense of PIR and PSI members. The PSI bureaucrats, however, were able to take advantage of their ethnic identity as "Samarinda-Banjarese" so that they were not driven out of office entirely. They held low-ranking jobs, waiting for a time when they could take revenge against the PNI-dominated bureaucracy. In fact, their opportunity for revenge came after the fall of Muis Hassan in 1966. Although they were relegated to meager positions by Muis Hassan, these PSI bureaucrats did not want to join forces with Soeharjo whom they considered too radical for their taste.

When President Sukarno made his declaration of Confrontation against Malaysia in 1963, Soeharjo undertook to lead East Kalimantan with his strong revolutionary spirit. Located strategically on the borders of both Sarawak and Sabah, East Kalimantan was to be placed under the military control of the Pepelrada (Pembantu Pelaksana Dwikora Daerah, the Regional Holder of the Dwikora Command) in which Soeharjo was

---

143 PT Mahakam was formed in 1952 by the I. A. Muis family. In 1954 it was able to obtain sailing routes to East Kalimantan. With three ships, it sailed to Balikpapan, Samarinda, and Tarakan. Due to bad management it went bankrupt, and by 1976 it only owned one ship. Its shipping route was taken over by PT Nagah Berlian, a company owned by a Lampung-bom Chinese, Ang Tiauw Bie. Ang has been able to profit from the great need for shipping services fueled by the timber boom. For a detailed discussion of the shipping industry, see Howard Dick, "The Indonesian Interisland Shipping Industry: A Case Study in Competition and Regulation" (PhD dissertation, The Australian National University, 1977), p. 143 and pp. 180-83.

the Panglima. The emergency power given to Soeharjo had made it possible for him to arrest all his political opponents. Moreover, he was supported in his efforts by the new police commander of East Kalimantan (Pangdak), Brigadier General Drs. Sumartono, and the commander of the Navy Station in Tarakan, Lieutenant Colonel Sudirman. Both men were strong supporters of President Sukarno's Confrontation and initiated several incursions into Sabah in 1964 and early 1965 under the coordination of Soeharjo.[144]

The military side of the Confrontation in East Kalimantan was not highly important. With only three battalions of its own, Kodam Mulawarman could only maintain border posts in places such as Nunukan, Malinau and Longnawang. Unlike in West Kalimantan, where the strong Brigade Mondau was assembled under Brigadier General Supardjo,[145] forces in East Kalimantan were never of brigade strength. Several platoons of paratroops (RPKAD) were stationed along the borders but they were put under Soeharjo's command. Thus, there were no RPKAD officers with key troops under their own command to rival the leadership of Soeharjo in East Kalimantan.

Since incursions across the land border were quite difficult, infiltrations took place mostly under the supervision of the KKO (Marines) at Nunukan. Furthermore, after the declaration of Dwikora (People's Two Commands) in May 1964 battalions of volunteers were sent to East Kalimantan. However, those volunteers did not really work as auxiliary troops. Most of them were given jobs as teachers in the interior of East Kalimantan, establishing strong rapport with the Dayak people.

While the military side of Confrontation was less apparent in East

---

144 For the complaints leveled by the Malaysian government over the Indonesian intrusions, see *Indonesian Involvement in Eastern Malaysia* (Kuala Lumpur: Malaysian Ministry of External Affairs, 1964), pp. 16-20. It should be noted that the KKO (Marines) launched an infiltration from Nunukan. The police have had a strong Mobile Brigade battalion in East Kalimantan since the 1950s for the purpose of operating against Ibnu Hadjar's Kesatuan Rakjat Jang Tertindas (KRJT) rebels in the Pasir and Pagatan areas. See also J.A.C. Mackie, *Konfrontasi: The Indonesia-Malaysia Dispute, 1963-1966* (Kuala Lumpur: Oxford University Press, 1974), pp. 200-75. Also George McT. Kahin, "Malaysia and Indonesia," *Pacific Affairs* (Fall 1964): 253-70. For the Indonesian view, see *Gelora Konfrontasi Menggandjang Malaysia* (Jakarta: Department of Foreign Affairs, 1964), p. 6.

145 Brigadier General Supardjo was to become the leader of the G-30-S Affair as the vice chairman of the "Revolutionary Council." He was executed by the army in 1968 after an Extra Ordinary Military Court (*Mahmilub*) proceeding.

than in West Kalimantan, where fighting was taking place on the border with Sarawak, the political atmosphere it created did have a substantial impact in the East as well. As a distant relative of First Vice Premier Dr. Subandrio, Soeharjo was able to use the strategic importance of East Kalimantan for his own political advancement. Soeharjo was considered a protégé of President Sukarno himself. Accordingly, he reported first to the President when he went to Jakarta rather than to either the Chief of Staff, General Yani, or to the Minister of Defense, General Nasution.[146] In fact, Soeharjo's relations with General Yani reached such a low point that it is believed that in 1965 Yani himself decided to relieve Soeharjo of his job and send him to the Army Staff College in Moscow.[147]

Despite the opposition towards him from the Samarinda Banjarese (including those with PNI, PSI, and Islamic leanings) and the aristocracy, Soeharjo was quite popular among the East Kalimantan people, especially the various Dayak groups in the interior. He led a modest life in Balikpapan and was known for his puritanical behavior, especially his lack of womanizing. He never rode a car (*sedan*) and traveled in his old Russian-made jeep. He was remembered as the only Pangdam who had traveled throughout East Kalimantan using *perahu* as well as land transportation.[148] To the *pejuang* and to his troops, Soeharjo was the personification of a real revolutionary leader: honest, austere, and attentive to his *anak buah* (followers) and the people. Such virtues had made him quite memorable among the *pejuang* of East Kalimantan who saw his political actions as a kind of *perjuangan* (struggle).

By early 1964, the Confrontation campaign had gained the necessary momentum for Soeharjo to undertake radical measures. In January 1964 the British oil company, PT Shell Indonesia, was taken over by the Kesatuan

---

146 Interview with General Nasution, July 14, 1979.

147 Soeharjo was in Moscow when the G-30-S Affair occurred. However, contrary to many reports, Soeharjo was apparently not involved in the Affair. He did not report to the Embassy in Moscow after finishing his course and was considered a deserter. (Interviews with Harun Nafsi, Samarinda, June 20, 1979; Abdul Muis Hassan, July 12, 1979; and General Nasution, July 14, 1979.) Having been persuaded by then Foreign Minister Adam Malik, R. Soeharjo returned to Indonesia in January 1977.

148 He is described in **Sejarah Kodam Mulawarman**, p. 25, as the only Pangdam to travel by foot in the interior of Kutai and Bulungan. (Also corroborated in interviews with Husein Jusuf, June 7, 1979; Harun Nafsi, June 20, 1979, and Abdulmutalib, June 23, 1979.) According to Abdulmutalib, Soeharjo was at that time still friendly with the PSI leaders in Samarinda, despite the banning of the PSI by the central government in 1960.

Aksi Buruh Minyak (Oil Workers United Front) as part of an anti-British campaign. In Balikpapan, the oil workers were mostly members of Perbum, while the PNI-affiliated Kesatuan Buruh Marhaenis played a minor role. The oil workers' leaders were put in charge of the company until President Sukarno intervened and placed the management of the company under Indonesian white collar managers. The participation of Perbum leaders in the oil company's management gave them the funds needed to undertake radical political activities that were in line with Soeharjo's policies in East Kalimantan.[149]

Hence by early 1964, Soeharjo had consolidated his power in East Kalimantan with the solid support of the army, the *pejuang* in Balikpapan and Samarinda, and the oil workers. His activities on behalf of the army and Sukarno's Confrontation campaign had given him national stature as a *pejuang* leader.[150] Such stature got another boost when President Sukarno convened all the Pangdam in Jakarta on March 17, 1964. On that occasion, Sukarno spoke of the British scenarios on the Confrontation, providing documents taken from the British Embassy. It was part of the beginning of a new stage in the Confrontation campaign. At this conference, the President also proclaimed the founding of *sukarelawan* (volunteers) corps to fight against Malaysia. Soeharjo went back to East Kalimantan full of "fighting spirit" against Malaysia.[151]

After his return Soeharjo acted quickly. In April 1964, he reportedly found a document which appeared to prove that the Bulungan aristocracy had ties to Malaysia, in that it stated that these aristocrats would proclaim merger with Sabah, Malaysia. Prior to Confrontation members of the Bulungan aristocracy had visited Sabah frequently because they had blood ties with the Sabah aristocrats that went as far back as the Sulu sultanate. Soeharjo feared that the Bulungan aristocrats could well become

---

149 For some reports on this, see **Bintang Timur** (Jakarta), January 21 and March 1, 1964. It was believed that Soeharjo's anti-British attitude resulted from his mistreatment at the hands of the British troops in Surabaya during the battle of Surabaya, which included physical abuse. (Personal communication from Benedict R.O'G. Anderson.) Soeharjo, however, explained his attitude toward PT Shell Indonesia as stemming from his nationalist feelings and his desire to help the workers. (Interview with R. Soeharjo, December 17, 1984.)

150 See for example, a report in **Bintang Timur**, March 6, 1964, on how Colonel Soeharjo and Brigadier General Rukman, Deputy Kasad (Army Chief of Staff) for East Indonesia "have escaped from the attacks of British planes."

151 See **Bintang Timur**, March 12, 17, and 18, 1964.

Malaysia's "fifth column" should the British troops attack Indonesia as was widely rumored. His fear was shared by the commander of Tarakan naval station, Lieutenant Colonel Sudirman. Their common objective was to establish a strong frontier in Bulungan where the Sukarelawan Tempur Dwikora (Auxiliary Troops of the Dwikora campaign), already assembled in Jakarta under a Brawijaya officer, Colonel Sabirin Mochtar, would be posted.

The discovery of arms in the former palace of the Sultan in the third week of April 1964 provided the pretext for the purge of the Bulungan aristocrats, although there had previously been doubts about the truth of allegations questioning their loyalty.[152] On April 24, Soeharjo ordered his troops stationed in Tanjung Selor to arrest all members of the Bulungan aristocracy. The aristocrats were separated into several groups. All the male members were put into one group and into one boat, while the women and children were placed in a separate boat. They were supposed to be transported first to Tarakan and from there taken to Balikpapan. This plan never materialized. Off the shore of Tarakan, all of them, about 30 persons in total, were gunned down by their own guards from Kodim Bulungan. Their bodies were thrown into the sea.

Although there are several differing accounts of this incident, all of them agree on the number of persons involved and the brutality of the killings.[153] Within the immediate family of Sultan Bulungan, only two sons survived because they had been able to escape at the time of the arrests. They fled to Sabah. Another son of the late Sultan Bulungan was summoned by Soeharjo from his school in Malang. Upon his arrival in Balikpapan, he was arrested and was never heard of again.[154]

---

152 The finding of the arms cache itself became a source of controversy. Most anti-Soeharjo groups, believed that Soeharjo himself had engineered the whole arms cache incident as a pretext to move against the Bulungan aristocracy. The *pejuang* who were sympathetic to Soeharjo, considered the finding of the arms cache as possibly true, given the relations between the Bulungan and Sabah aristocrats. (Interviews with Abdul Muis Hassan, Husein Jusuf, Harun Nafsi, and Anang Sulaiman.)

153 Most accounts state that 30 persons were killed. This figure was provided by Hiefnie Effendy, a prominent journalist in Samarinda since the 1950s. In contrast, the aristocratic groups tended to place the death toll at as high a figure as 77. Interviews with AR Padmo, June 25, 1979, and Hiefnie Effendy.

154 Anang Sulaiman, who was the representative of PT Mahakam in Malang at that time, has stated that "[he felt] guilty because [he had given] him the ticket to Balikpapan." (Interview with Anang Sulaiman, June 16, 1979.)

This killing of the Bulungan aristocrats came to be known locally as the Bultikan affair. It was widely believed that it was directed by Soeharjo himself. Even his fellow Brawijaya successor, General Sumitro has acknowledged that Soeharjo himself directed the actions.[155] However, there have been many different opinions regarding the motives and reasons underlying the purge.

For most Samarinda Banjarese, especially those from the PNI group, the Bulungan affair was only the worst example of Soeharjo's ruthlessness. They believed that in an effort to consolidate his power, he had overstepped his mandate and used the finding of the arms as a pretext to further his objective of eliminating the East Kalimantan aristocrats. While not particularly fond of the aristocracy, the Samarinda Banjarese did not appreciate Soeharjo's violent attacks against them. Soeharjo's allegation that the aristocrats were Malaysian agents was categorized by the Samarinda Banjarese as a *post-facto* justification of the killings.

On the other hand, the *pejuang* tended to support Soeharjo's accusations. They believed that the Bulungan aristocrats were trying to recapture their lost power by aligning themselves with a foreign power, a tactic which historically had quite often been pursued by commercial aristocracies elsewhere. Although the *pejuang* questioned the appropriateness and the necessity of the killings, they could accept them as a necessary cost of the Confrontation policy. In such a charged political atmosphere, the silent killing of the Bulungan aristocrats was considered an outgrowth of the radicalization the Confrontation policy had fostered.

The affair itself received little attention outside East Kalimantan. Indeed, even within East Kalimantan few protested against Soeharjo's move, as the Bulungan aristocrats were not widely known. Having lived only in Bulungan the aristocracy did not have any connections with the powerful bureaucracy in Samarinda nor marriage alliances with other aristocracies. Hence, when they were killed, there were no outside supporters who could protest Soeharjo's actions. Political groups such as the Samarinda PNI simply watched on quietly. Even the army headquarters, Mabad, (Markas Besar Angkatan Darat) which did not

---

155 Soeharjo's successor, the then Brigadier General Sumitro, has acknowledged the occurrence of "silent killings," although he emphasized that these killings had occurred as part of the general tense climate of Confrontation. (Interview with General Sumitro, May 7, 1978.)

always agree with Soeharjo, did not dare to take punitive actions against him, because he was a rising star within the political context engendered by Guided Democracy.

By May 1964, Soeharjo had become a celebrity in the left-wing politics of Guided Democracy, bearing the image of a popular general who could be counted on to provide a revolutionary kind of leadership. Indeed, Yani's leadership within the army was seen as the counterpoint to Soeharjo's populist and dynamic leadership style. His success at the Afro-Asian Film Festival held in Jakarta in late April added further to his revolutionary leadership credentials among the political elite of Jakarta. He won the "Lumumba Award" for best direction while his film, "Tangan-Tangan Yang Kotor" [Dirty Hands] won the Bandung award, the highest award of the festival.[156] His national reputation as well as his strong backing from Jakarta's elite, particularly from President Sukarno, the Indonesian Communist Party, and the Indonesian Party (Partindo) added to his power at the provincial level.

With his increased power, Soeharjo was ready to strike a decisive blow against the *pejuangs'* arch-enemy, the Kutai aristocracy. Soeharjo decided to strike against them in August 1964. Since *kabupaten* Kutai was located outside the first military defense line, a mass arrest of the aristocrats could not easily be justified on the basis of the aristocrats forming a "fifth column." Soeharjo, however, was easily able to find another pretext. He accused the Kutai aristocrats of attempting to revive the *swapraja*. Soeharjo's troops were sent to Tenggarong where they arrested prominent members of the Kutai aristocracy, including Sultan Parikesit, his half-brother and former Governor, Pranoto, the Bupati of Kutai, Aji Raden Padmo, and the chairman of the Kutai DPRD, a PNI man named Mansjursjah. They were put in a temporary jail within the military compound in Balikpapan. Pranoto was also accused of mishandling the provincial budget and embezzling several million rupiah. Although the accusation proved to be true, it was generally believed that Pranoto was not personally taking the funds for himself.[157] However, Pranoto, alone,

---

156 See **Bintang Timur**, May 2, 1964.
157 Interviews with Abdul Muis Hassan, Harun Nafsi, and Oemar Dachlan. According to Abdul Muis Hassan, Pranoto was guilty of mismanaging 13 million *rupiah* of governmental funds. Harun Nafsi believes that the mismanagement of this large sum of government funds was

was sent to the feared-RTM (Military Detention Center) in Jakarta, where he eventually died.[158]

In addition to putting Parikesit and Padmo in Balikpapan's jail, Soeharjo further humiliated the Kutai aristocracy by burning publicly the celebrated attributes of the Sultan. In front of supporting spectators, Soeharjo ordered the burning of the Sultan's clothes in the yard of Tenggarong Palace. His plan to burn the palace, as he had done in Bulungan, was prevented by Muis Hassan, who sent Banjarese police to protect the building.[159] Soeharjo was an appreciative spectator of the burning of the Sultan's attributes, witnessing the event from a boat in the Mahakam River. A young Javanese *pamong praja*, Drs. Roesdibjono was chosen to replace Padmo as the Bupati of Kutai. Hence, Soeharjo fulfilled the old dream of the *pejuang* of taking over and destroying the Kutai aristocracy.

Soeharjo's power continued to increase in the second half of 1964 and early 1965. He headed the provincial leadership of *Panca Tunggal* (Five Regional Bodies) over Governor Muis Hassan who was only a member of that body.[160] It was headquartered in Balikpapan where the other members of *Panca Tunggal*, the Pangdak (Regional Police Chief), Jaksa Tinggi (Regional Prosecutor), and chairman of the Front Nasional, resided. Balikpapan thereby reached the strongest position it would ever have in its rivalry with Samarinda for the political leadership of East Kalimantan.

However, Muis Hassan was able to continue as Governor, despite increasing pressure from Soeharjo to put more military officers into the provincial bureaucracy. With strong support from the PNI Central Board

---

probably mainly due to Pranoto's practice of giving away government funds to his friends and allies as had been done in the old days of the Kutai sultanate. According to Nafsi, Pranoto just gave money to friends he believed needed the money. Pranoto's widow is living a poor life, having had to rent a house in the poor section of Samarinda.

158 Pranoto died in prison because of prison conditions. (Interviews with Abdul Muis Hassan, Harun Nafsi, and Oemar Dachlan.)

159 Interviews with Hiefny Effendy, June 20, 1979 and Abdul Muis Hassan, July 12, 1979.

160 The Pane Tunggal was also part of Guided Democracy's scheme for the incorporation of the PKI into the provincial leadership through the work of the PKI-affiliated Front Nasional leaders at the provincial level. However, in East Kalimantan, the Front National was represented mostly by Harun Nafsi, a PSII-leader. Yet, Fahrul Baraqbah, a PKI leader, sometimes used his position within the Front Nasional to enhance his leadership. (Interview with Harun Nafsi, June 20, 1979.)

and President Sukarno himself, Muis Hassan was to survive Soeharjo's reign. From 1962 onwards, he had expanded the PNI's influence throughout the bureaucracy down to the *kecamatan* (subdistrict) level where it was estimated that about 75 percent of the *camat* (subdistrict heads) were PNI members or sympathizers.[161]

At the *kabupaten* level, Soeharjo was able to appoint his own men as Bupati and mayors at the expense of the PNI. Accordingly, in Balikpapan, the PNI *pamong praja* bureaucrat of Kutai origin, A.R.S. Mohammad, was replaced as mayor by an army officer of Banjarese origin, Major Zaenal Arifin, a member of Soeharjo's entourage. Similarly, in Samarinda, Soeharjo replaced his fellow-Brawijaya mayor, Captain Sudjono AJ, with his own man, Major Ngoedio from the Military Court in Balikpapan. And, in Berau, Soeharjo appointed another Kodam officer, Captain Djajadi, as Bupati, replacing the former head of the Berau aristocracy, Aji Raden Ajub. Soeharjo's policy of appointing his own men as Bupati and mayors enabled him to undermine Muis Hassan's authority by early 1965. While Muis Hassan could claim that he dominated the Governor's office and the *camat*, it was Soeharjo who controlled the Bupati and mayors. Therefore, in all likelihood, Soeharjo was moving in a direction where he might have been able to put his own man in as Governor in 1965, had he himself not been replaced as Pangdam in March of that year.

Soeharjo's replacement was more the result of national political considerations than a response to provincial resentment against him. By becoming a favorite general of Sukarno, Subandrio, and the left-wing parties in Jakarta (most notably the PKI and Partindo), Soeharjo had put himself in direct conflict with the Army Chief of Staff, General Ahmad Yani. Yani had always been unhappy not only with Soeharjo's leadership but also with his free dealing with Sukarno and Subandrio over Yani's head. Moreover, Soeharjo's emphasis on the issue of Confrontation was in direct contrast with Yani's policy of playing it down in order to reduce the power of the PKI. Hence, Yani saw Soeharjo as playing into the PKI's hands in its increasing competition with the army, and so, planned to replace Soeharjo with his own man, also from the Brawijaya division,

---

161 Interviews with Sjahrumsjah Idris and Anang Sulaiman, both chairmen of East Kalimantan's PNI branch since the 1960s, June 16 and 18, 1979.

Brigadier General Sumitro.

By appointing the anti-Communist Sumitro, Yani was trying to halt the progress of the PKI in East Kalimantan while preserving the interests of the army. Hence, Sumitro reduced the support that the Kodam had given to the PKI, and, especially, to its union, Perbum. Moreover, while maintaining the Kodam's public posture with regard to the Confrontation policy, Sumitro was quite cautious in embarking on any military venture against Malaysia. He was to follow the policy of the army leadership in Jakarta, aimed at preventing the PKI from using the Malaysia campaign for its own purposes.

While retreating from Soeharjo's policy of close relations with the PKI and his vigorous anti-Malaysian campaign, Sumitro did not dismiss most of Soeharjo's appointees who, like him, were Brawijaya officers. Although Sumitro differed from Soeharjo in his attitude towards the PKI, he shared a similar revolutionary spirit with regard to the aristocracy and the non-*pejuang*. To this end, Sumitro took over the leadership of Balikpapan's *pejuang* from Soeharjo, especially with regard to its competition with the Samarinda-based PNI.

Although his tenure as Pangdam was quite short, only nine months, Sumitro's leadership was very important in determining the future of East Kalimantan politics. By containing the progress of the PKI, Sumitro was able to prevent a build up of political tensions during 1965. Consequently, by the time of the September 30 Movement (G-30-S), Sumitro was easily able to arrest the prominent leaders of the PKI and Perbum without much intervention from the other political parties. He also arrested fellow Brawijaya officers who were known to be close to the PKI, all of whom were Soeharjo's appointees. In doing so, Sumitro was largely able to prevent in East Kalimantan the kind of bloodshed that the G-30-S Affair produced elsewhere in Indonesia.

When Sumitro was promoted to the position of the Assistant for Operations of the Mabad Army Chief of Staff in Jakarta, Colonel Soekadijo became leader of Kodam in Balikpapan. A Brawijaya officer, like Soeharjo and Sumitro, Soekadijo could command the loyalty of Kodam officers, most of whom originated from the important Brawijaya division. Brigadier General Mung Parhadimuljo, also from the Brawijaya, was appointed as Sumitro's successor, but he had spent most of his life in the RPKAD and was considered a political general.[162] Thus, Soekadijo took over the political leadership of the army in East Kalimantan in the confusing months following the G-30-S Affair.

The G-30-S Affair had a considerable adverse impact on the power of the army in East Kalimantan, especially with regard to its officers who were in civilian jobs. All of the army's Bupati and mayors, as well as many of its Kodim commanders were arrested.[163] They were placed in a military jail in Balikpapan. However, since Sumitro was a Brawijaya man, he was easily able to replace them with other officers from that division. Hence, the ranks of Kodam Mulawarman remained dominated by Brawijaya officers.

Moreover, this decline in the army's power had its civilian parallel in the provincial bureaucracy in Samarinda. The PNI's control over the provincial bureaucracy since 1960 had stimulated the growth of a group within the Banjarese community who were strongly opposed to the PNI. Most of the members of this Banjarese group came from Masjumi, PSI, and HMI backgrounds. They not only resented the PNI's domination of the bureaucracy, but also its domination of academic life. By that time, a new generation of university-educated people with Islamic leanings had emerged from the Banjarese community in Samarinda.

Prior to the emergence of this new university-educated generation, the Islamic organizations in Samarinda, such as NU and Muhammadiyah, had strong ties with Banjarmasin from where many of their leaders were recruited.[164] In the early 1960s, through the IAIN in Banjarmasin, Islamic organizations in Samarinda were able to form a branch of IAIN in Samarinda. For the first time, together with the students of the state university, Universitas Mulawarman, the Islamic-leaning Banjarese in Samarinda were to have their own educated elite. The HMI (Islamic Students Organization) was soon to compete with the GMNI (PNI

---

162 For a brief biography of Mung Parhadimuljo, see Biographical Appendix in this monograph.

163 Those who were arrested included the Mayor of Balikpapan, Lieutenant Colonel Bambang Sutikno; the Kodim of Balikpapan, Lieutenant Colonel Tony Sukartono; and the Fifth Assistant to the Pangdam who was also the Secretary of the Provincial Front Nasional, Colonel Rusmono. The former Kodim of Samarinda, Lieutenant Colonel Sudjono, was also jailed, as well as the Bupati of Pasir, Lieutenant Colonel Sujatmo.

164 For the origins of the Islamic movements in East Kalimantan and their ties to Banjarmasin, see Taufik, "Perkembangan." In contrast, the secular organizations such as the PNI, PSI, and PIR had established direct relations with their headquarters in Jakarta.

student organization) for the domination of Mulawarman University.

In various universities in Java, students from East Kalimantan had established their own organization, KPMKT (Keluarga Pelajar Mahasiswa Kalimantan Timur -- Family of Students from East Kalimantan). It was dominated by HMI members and students coming from Islamic backgrounds. Most of them did not get fellowships from the provincial government, since the provincial government fellowships were mostly given to the children of PNI leaders. Hence, they resented the PNI leadership in Samarinda, not least because they saw no career chance for themselves within the power structure that leadership headed. Moreover, at the KPMKT national board in Jakarta many students of Banjarese origins were playing important roles in the national student movements of KAMI (Kesatuan Aksi Mahasiswa Indonesia, Indonesian Student Action United Group) and KAPPI (Kesatuan Aksi Pemuda Pelajar Indonesia, Indonesian Secondary School Students and Youth United Group). In line with the growing political polarization of Guided Democracy, these KPMKT students actively confronted the PNI-affiliated GMNI both at the national and provincial political levels. Hence, the children of the Samarinda Islamic groups were in the forefront of student organizations prior to the G-30-S Affair.

Moreover, in the early months of the post-coup period, Samarinda was flooded with South Kalimantan's student leaders who took refuge in East Kalimantan from a heavy-handed pro-Sukarno Regional Commander, Brigadier General Sabirin Mochtar. A Brawijaya officer like Soeharjo, Sabirin Mochtar was known for his harsh measures against the KAMI-KAPPI students. He was very active in the campaign against Malaysia and was once the head of the Sukarelawan Tempur Dwikora. The arrival of the Banjarmasin student leaders also laid the groundwork for ending the PNI's political dominance in Samarinda.

In the aftermath of the G-30-S Affair, these student organizations formed the Samarinda branches of KAMI and KAPPI, under the leadership of non-GMNI students. Regional Commander Mung Parhadimuljo himself was quite sympathetic to the students, as the RPKAD troops had been in Jakarta. Since the power to grant and to stop demonstrations rested in the hands of the Kodam as the Laksus Kopkamtib for East Kalimantan, the regional command used this power to settle its account with the provincial political leadership in Samarinda. The students, became one of the components of the political game skillfully played by Parhadimuljo's Chief of Staff, Colonel Soekadijo, who wanted the governorship for himself. Thus the KAMI-KAPPI students in Samarinda were granted considerable freedom in holding demonstrations and public rallies.

The target of the student demonstrations was Governor Muis Hassan and his PNI-dominated provincial bureaucracy. Since he had opposed the PKI's domination and influence, he could not be considered a pro-Communist Governor. However, with the increasing anti-Sukarno tone at the national level, Muis Hassan was accused of having had close relations with Sukarno and was labeled a Sukarnoist.

When Sukarno was removed from the actual power of the Presidency by the army in March 1966, student demonstrations demanding the dismissal of Governor Muis Hassan increased in East Kalimantan. The political slogan was changed from "anti G-30-S" to "anti *Orde Lama* (Old Order)," causing many Governors to resign. By the end of 1966, Muis Hassan bowed to political pressure and refused the offer of the then Minister of Interior, Basuki Rachmat, to remain in office for a while longer.[165] It should be noted that while the PNI members were strong enough at the regional level to stage counter demonstrations, they refrained from doing so, due to the party's decline at the national level.

Basuki Rachmat then appointed his fellow Brawijaya officer, Colonel Soekadijo, as Acting Governor for East Kalimantan. Although he had the support of the Pangdam Mung and the Kodam bureaucracy, Soekadijo was not well placed politically at the provincial level due to his past role as Soeharjo's deputy. Hence, he was soon opposed by the non-PNI Banjarese groups in Samarinda who resented the possibility of the appointment of a Javanese Governor.

It was in this critical situation that the KPMKT proved the usefulness of its political network in the important cities of Java. In view of the increasing power of the military in post-coup Indonesia, the KPMKT realized that it had to oppose the appointment of Colonel Soekadijo

---

165 Interview with Abdul Muis Hassan, July 12, 1979. According to him, Basuki Rachmat proposed that he take the job of Deputy Governor in order to get the cooperation of the mostly PNI bureaucrats. However, Abdul Muis Hassan rejected this offer. He was most influenced in this decision by his wife who was irritated by the demonstrations against him, and preferred to live in Jakarta.

with the candidacy of another military officer. A candidate was found in the person of Colonel Wahab Sjahranie, then Deputy Assistant for Functional Affairs to the Kasad in Jakarta. Colonel Sjahranie came from an aristocratic Banjarese family in Rantau, South Kalimantan. Although he came from South Kalimantan, he could well be considered a *"putra daerah"* (native son) of Banjarese-dominated East Kalimantan. He had spent most of his army career as a teacher at SESKOAD in Bandung so that he became the chairman of the Infantry Department before he was called to Army Headquarters. Prior to the war, he was a *pamong praja* official, working as a *camat* in South Kalimantan.[166]

While he was close to the Kasad and General Panggabean, he was also a close associate of the powerful commander of SESKOAD, Lieutenant General Suwarto. Hence, he was better placed politically at the national level than Soekadijo. Moreover, Sjahranie was a more attractive candidate at the regional level because the demands for a *putra daerah* for Governor were too strong to be resisted by the central government. Wahab Sjahranie, then, was a welcome candidate to the non-PNI Banjarese of Samarinda, for by taking over the Governorship he removed the possibility of Soekadijo, a Javanese, assuming that position.

The ethnic dimensions of the competition over the Governorship could not be taken lightly in the aftermath of the G-30-S Affair in East Kalimantan. For the non-*pejuang* Banjarese, Soeharjo's past leadership had shown the dangers that a Javanese leader would pose in the increasingly competitive atmosphere between the Banjarese and the Javanese in East Kalimantan. Javanese migrants had come to East Kalimantan in large numbers, due mostly to the Confrontation campaign and to Perbum's activities in Tarakan and Balikpapan. In the aftermath of the G-30-S Affair, many of these migrants fell victim to the charge that they had a left-wing political orientation. A large number of them were jailed as activists of Perbum and the PKI. It was only because the Kodam was led by fellow Javanese that these migrants were able to escape physical abuse. Hence, it was in the migrants' best interests that the Governorship be in the hands of a fellow Javanese. Furthermore, a Javanese Governor might

---

166 For a brief biography of Abdul Wahab Sjahranie, see Biographical Appendix and **Buku MPR 1971**, pp. 758-59.

also provide more avenues and incentives for the economic and social advancement of the Javanese. It was precisely because of this possibility that the Banjarese of Samarinda had insisted on their fellow Banjarese becoming Governor in order to protect them from the incoming Javanese migrants in the province. In the end, the Banjarese got what they wanted and Colonel Wahab Sjahranie was appointed as the new Governor of East Kalimantan in 1967.

CHAPTER SIX
THE TIMBER BOOM AND THE CENTRALIZATION OF POWER

The governorship of Abdul Wahab Sjahranie was characterized by East Kalimantan's emergence as the leading timber exporter in Indonesia. Under the easy terms of the Foreign Investment Law No. 1/1967, timber came to be exploited on a huge scale, especially between 1967 and 1970. The timber boom produced far-reaching changes in the social and economic fabric of the region. In the first place, it encouraged a large wave of migrants to East Kalimantan. These migrants came from other parts of Kalimantan, but also from Java and Sulawesi. Many Banjarese came in from South Kalimantan, taking advantage of the land communications to Balikpapan. These migrants were often peasants who simply left their lands to earn cash more easily as laborers in the timber camps.

Aside from the Banjarese, a large number of Javanese arrived in Samarinda seeking employment in the timber exploitation enterprises. They worked mostly in the timber camps and in the various service sector jobs available in Samarinda, Tarakan, and Balikpapan. The availability of easy transport, including log-carrier, from Surabaya to East Kalimantan made the journey quite short and cheap. This great influx of Javanese migrants not only changed considerably the ethnic composition of East Kalimantan, but also helped change the ethnic balance of power in the region. Whereas earlier the Banjarese were the dominant group in the cities of Balikpapan, Samarinda, and Tarakan, the arrival of new Javanese migrants seriously undermined their position of dominance.

The third group of migrants came from South Sulawesi, especially Pare-pare and the Mandar region where agricultural conditions were disrupted because of the long strife between the Kahar Muzakkar rebels and the army. With the introduction of motorized *perahu*, the migrants could reach Balikpapan in about 36 hours. Many then went further north to Tarakan and Bulungan, especially Nunukan, where a Buginese community had existed since the seventeenth century. Most of the Buginese who migrated to East Kalimantan came from the lower classes. A good number of educated Buginese, however, also came to the region looking for jobs at Mulawarman University; in fact, so many entered the university that the Buginese came to dominate two university faculties: the Faculty of Economy and the Faculty of Social Politics.

Additionally, a large number of Torajanese have also migrated to East Kalimantan, especially to Tarakan. Many of them now work for the timber companies, but some also pursue small trade activities.

The boom increased East Kalimantan's food supply dependence, and the new rice areas of Hulusungai were only too happy to send their produce to Balikpapan, together with other foods, such as vegetables and meat. The intensification of forest exploitation also forced many Dayak groups to settle in the urban centers, mostly in the *kecamatan* capitals. Already in the late 1960s, a sizable number of educated people from the various Dayak groups had emerged and were prepared to play important political roles in provincial politics. Tarakan was the main center for the Kayan-Kenyah group, and Samarinda for the interior Dayaks of Kutai *kabupaten*, such as the Tunjung, Bahau, and Benuaq.

Overall, this migration to East Kalimantan helped double the population of the province from a half million people in the middle of the 1960s to about 1 million by 1978 (see Table 5 for East Kalimantan's demographic changes).

From Table 5 we can see that the timber boom started around the area of Samarinda, where the population doubled between 1961 and 1971. Although Balikpapan's population had increased quite substantially in the late 1960s, the population expansion accelerated rapidly in more recent years, as the systematic exploitation of the forest developed there. It is striking that the boom has served to increase the percentage of people living in the urban centers; the cities of Samarinda, Balikpapan, and Tarakan together now constitute about 50 percent of the province's entire population.

The exact ethnic composition of this population increase is quite difficult to assess because of a lack of ethnic data in the national census. An educated guess, however, suggests the following: The Javanese still form the majority in Balikpapan (between 35 and 40 percent), followed by the Buginese (between 25 and 30 percent) and the Banjarese (about 20 percent). The rest of the population is mainly composed of various ethnic groups from North Sulawesi (Minahasans and Sangirese, about 5 percent) and others, including declining numbers of Chinese. Hence, while the Javanese maintain their prewar plurality, the Buginese now outnumber the Banjarese. Apparently most Banjarese migrants from South Kalimantan only stop over in Balikpapan before continuing their journey to Samarinda.[167]

The Banjarese, however, have maintained their prewar demographic dominance in Samarinda. They are estimated to constitute about 40 percent of the population, while the Javanese percentage has grown to about thirty. The Buginese demographic share has stayed put at about 10 percent, while another 10 percent of the population is divided between Chinese and various Dayak groups. It should be noted that "Banjarese" includes people of Melayu and Kutai backgrounds who have intermarried with the Banjarese since the 1950s.

In Tarakan the Javanese population share has jumped far ahead of the shares of the other ethnic groups, to the extent that they probably now constitute about 50 percent of the population. Buginese and Torajanese constitute about 20 percent, while the North Sulawesi groups and the Chinese each represent about 15 percent of the population. The Javanese have mainly come to work in oil-related businesses, while the Buginese and the Torajanese work in trade and agriculture. The Dayak groups are mostly concentrated in the *kecamatan* capitals of inland Bulungan, especially in Tanjung Palas, Kerayan, and Malinau.[168]

However, for the province as a whole, the Banjarese are still the politically dominant ethnic group, due mostly to their widespread representation in the *kecamatan* capitals along the Mahakam River as

---

167 The Banjarese from South Kalimantan have migrated mostly to Central and East Kalimantan. See Marliani Johansjah, "Mobilitas Penduduk di Kalimantan Selatan" (Fakultas Ekonomi, Universitas Lambung Mangkurat, 1979, Typescript), p. 4. Compare Johansjah's discussion with that of Hasan Basri concerning Banjarese migration to Java in the article, "Perpindahan Orang Banjar ke Surakarta: Kasus Migrasi Inter Etnis di Indonesia," in **Prisma** (Indonesian edition), number 3 (1988): 42-56.

168 See **Registrasi Penduduk Kalimantan Timur** (Samarinda: Bappeda Kalimantan Timur, 1978), p. 15.

early as the late nineteenth century. They may well constitute 30 percent of the provincial population, while the Javanese compose between 15 and 20 percent. Demographically, however, East Kalimantan is still predominantly a Dayak province. These Dayak groups, however, are largely fragmented along *anaksuku* (subgroup) lines and do not possess good means of communication among them. Their numbers are estimated at between 35 and 40 percent of the provincial population, most of them living in the *kabupaten* of Kutai and Bulungan.[169] The nature of the demographic and socio-economic changes in East Kalimantan worked in the long term to the advantage of the Javanese. Although not yet the majority, the Javanese have a very strong presence in the three important cities of the province. Occupational and educational differences among them are great. Some work as government officials and are temporarily stationed in Balikpapan, while many work as common laborers in the timber camps or as service sector employees in the cities. Yet together these varied occupational groups provide the strong Javanese constituency needed by Javanese officials at the provincial and Kodam levels to guard against the dominance of the Banjarese.

---

169 Ibid.

Table 5. Population changes in East Kalimantan

No.	Kabupaten/kotamadya	1961	1971	1977
1	Balikpapan	91,706	137,340	238,141
2	Samarinda	69,712	137,918	190,393
3	Kutai	220,256	241,412	315,209
4	Berau	28,256	31,954	38,726
5	Bulungan[a]	95,685	119,199	158,380
6	Pasir	44,967	57,192	67,719
Total	East Kalimantan	550,582	725,115	1,008,568

Sources: *Registrasi Penduduk Kalimantan Timur 1977* (Samarinda: Bappeda Kalimantan Timur, 1978), pp. 1-9.

Monografi Daerah Propinsi Kalimantan Timur 1967 (Samarinda: Kantor Gubernur Kalimantan Timur, 1968), jilid I, pp. 18-20.

Burhanuddin Zainal Abidin, "Beberapa Masalah Pengelolaan Proyek Transmigrasi dipropinsi Daerah Tingkat I Kalimantan Timur" (MA thesis, Universitas Mulawarman, 1976), p. 28.

[a] Including the *kecamatan* of Tarakan which in 1978 was designated as a *Kotamadya Administratif*. It is led by its own Walikota (Mayor) who, however, still reports to the Bupati of Bulungan. The population of Tarakan climbed from 31,118 in 1971 to 44,415 in 1977. Ibid.

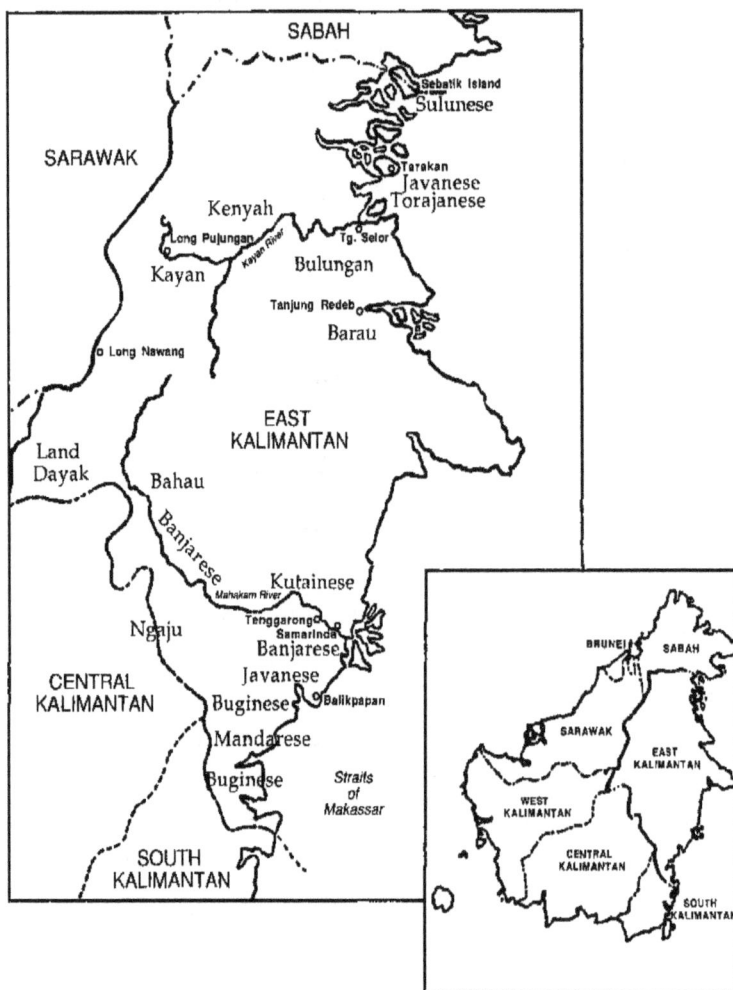

Map 4. Ethnic groups of East Kalimantan

It was in this demographic, political, and economic context that Governor Wahab Sjahranie ruled East Kalimantan from 1967 until 1978. At the time of his appointment, he had succeeded in winning the support of a variety of groups which traditionally had conflicting interests and had been out of power during the days of Muis Hassan and Soeharjo.

To run the provincial bureaucracy, Wahab Sjahranie replaced Muis Hassan's PNI men with two different types of bureaucrats. The first were the "PSI"-oriented Banjarese bureaucrats who had been put aside by Muis Hassan. They were now given important positions. Haji Kadrie Uning, a Samarinda-*pejuang*, for example, became the Mayor of Samarinda. Others such as Munadi Arief and Haji Rifaddin, got key jobs in the provincial bureaucracy.[170]

The second type of bureaucrat came from the Kutai aristocracy. A Banjarese aristocrat himself, Wahab Sjahranie used the Kutai aristocracy in order to ensure the "de-PNI-ization" of the provincial bureaucracy. He replaced the PNI Sekwilda Drs. Djakfar Achmad with Aji Raden Padmo, a top Kutai aristocrat just released from Soeharjo's jail. Other Kutai-Melayu aristocrats, such as Encik Mas Djakaria and A.R.S. Mohammad, were also given important positions later on, as Sekwilda (replacing Padmo) and Deputy Governor respectively.[171]

Hence the Kutai aristocrats experienced a limited revival during Wahab Sjahranie's governorship. They worked as high officials in the Governor's office, though the Bupati of Kutai remained Muis Hassan's appointee, Drs. Achmad Dahlan, a PNI-oriented Banjarese. The Kutai aristocrats, nonetheless, did not experience a full revival mainly because of the absence of any Kutai recruitment into the provincial bureaucracy between 1960 and 1965. Kutai interests were then still represented by the

---

170   Haji Encik Rifaddin was jailed by Soeharjo because of his Kutai connection. He was given the title "Encik" by the Sultan. Soeharjo did not like him because "he had forgotten his poor friends in Jakarta." (Interview with Abdulmutalib, June 23, 1979.) He was appointed Head of the Public Works Agency which controlled most governmental projects by Wahab Sjahranie. Another PSI *pamong praja*, Abdul Rasjid, was given a job as a special aide to the Governor, leading the PNI leaders to accuse Wahab Sjahranie of being "influenced by the PSI." Interviews with Sjahrumsjah Idris and Anang Sulaiman, June 16 and 18, 1979, respectively.

171   Interview with Encik Mas Djakaria, June 25, 1979. A.R.S. Mohammad was actually a member of the PNI but he was not considered a key figure in the Samarinda-based Banjarese group which had dominated the PNI in the early 1960s. Moreover, he was one of the few Kutai aristocrats who were available for appointment at a time when there was a very limited pool of Kutai aristocrats in the provincial government.

PIR-oriented OS VIA graduates who had worked with Pranoto, such as Padmo and Djakarta. Other prominent Kutai bureaucrats either preferred to live in Java (such as Aji Raden Afloes and Aji Raden Djokoprawiro) or had been discredited by their involvement with the Masjumi (such as Aji Kariowiti).

At the same time, the younger generation of Kutai aristocrats rarely came back to East Kalimantan because of the anti-aristocratic climate of the pre-1966 period. Although many of them got university degrees, they preferred to live in Jakarta where their aristocratic background was not a disadvantage. Those who did go back to East Kalimantan were mostly from the lower aristocracy of Awang origins, who had political ties with the PNI. It is true that many of them had middle level jobs at the provincial and *kabupaten* levels, but their positions were not that important.

Seen in this light, Soeharjo's anti-aristocratic purge was decisive in preventing the internal regeneration of the Kutai aristocrats within the bureaucracy. They had been so humiliated by Soeharjo's policies that most of the more enterprising younger aristocrats now worked and lived outside East Kalimantan. The long-term effect of Soeharjo's purge then is quite comparable to the impact of the *revolusi sosial* (social revolution) in East Sumatra, after which the local aristocratic groups were foreclosed from controlling the provincial leadership. Hence, despite all his efforts, Wahab Sjahranie proved unable substantially to recreate the Kutai aristocracy's old bureaucratic power. Only the lower aristocracy of Awangs benefitted from the absence of high Kutai aristocrats in the bureaucracy, for they could now claim to represent the Kutais at a time of increasing power struggles between the Javanese and the Banjarese.

Aside from the PSI-Banjarese and PIR-Kutai bureaucrats, Wahab Sjahranie also brought in his own "kitchen-cabinet," composed mostly of Banjarese from South Kalimantan. Some of them were military officers while others were civilian officials, yet all had worked with Sjahranie in the prewar period when he was a *pamong praja* and during his postwar military career.[172] Their presence caused great resentment among the

---

172 Among those who came with Wahab Sjahranie were the head of the Social Political Bureau, Colonel Said Sjeh and the Governor's spokesman, Abdurrachman Musa. The head of Pertamina in Balikpapan, Colonel Burhan Daniel, and the head of the Ferry and River Traffic Agency, Lieutenant Colonel Anwar Beck, during Sjahranie's tenure in office had been fellow guerrillas of

Samarinda-Banjarese bureaucrats, who had been suspicious of the South Kalimantan Banjarese ever since colonial times.

Wahab Sjahranie was not only able to consolidate his power within the bureaucracy, but was also able to end the PNI's domination of political life through the use of various coalitions. At first, he maintained close relations with the leaderships of the KAMI, KAPPI, and KPMKT who had helped him come to power. The young leaders of KAMI were recruited into the government-supported political organization, Golkar, while many graduates of the KPMKT were given jobs in the provincial bureaucracy. The political leaders of KAMI and KPMKT were mostly Banjarese, from both Banjarmasin and Samarinda. They were to constitute a counterforce to the young generation of PNI *sarjana* who now were shunted aside in the provincial bureaucracy.

Wahab Sjahranie was quick to use the resentment of non-PNI political parties to consolidate his power in the DPRDGR. He also developed a coalition among these small parties to counter the power of the military officers of Kodam origins, since he had not yet established his own political apparatus within Golkar. Hence, parties such as IPKI, Murba, and PSII always supported Wahab Sjahranie prior to the consolidation of Golkar in 1970.

By the time of the general election in 1971, Wahab Sjahranie had been able to put his supporters into the leadership of DPRDGR. A former member of the South Kalimantan-based guerrilla forces himself, Wahab Sjahranie was able to enlist the support of the *pejuang* in both Balikpapan and Samarinda. These *pejuang* saw in him a chance to defeat their old rivals in the Samarinda-based PNI while still maintaining their Banjarese-ness at a time when the Javanese constituted a growing political threat.

By 1968 Sjahranie had installed a Samarinda *pejuang*, Mohammad Sabrie, as chairman of the provincial DPRDGR replacing Major Supeno, a Brawijaya officer from Kodam Mulawarman who had been appointed by Colonel Soekadijo.[173] Sabrie was a former member of Murba and, with him, the whole leadership of Murba in Samarinda eventually moved into Golkar. Sabrie's deputy was an IPKI man, Siel Stekanggen, from the Ngaju

---

Wahab Sjahranie from the ALRI Divisi IV, South Kalimantan.

173 For a brief biography of Mohammad Sabrie, see Biographical Appendix and **Buku MPR 1971**, p. 960.

Dayak ethnic group in Central Kalimantan. Stekanggen was to continue his support for Sjahranie by joining Golkar in the 1971 election.[174]

The collapse of the PNI also encouraged two important political segments of the Dayak community to emerge. The first group came from the interior of Kutai itself and belonged to the Bahau-Tunjung-Benuaq complex of Dayak peoples. Catholic missionaries had started activities in that area in the early 1950s, soon after the dissolution of the Kutai sultanate. (Before that, the Dutch had promised the Sultan that no missionary would be allowed to operate within the Kutai realm.) By the mid 1960s, the first graduates of Catholic elementary schools were finishing their university education in various places outside East Kalimantan, such as in Yogyakarta and in Banjarmasin.

By 1966, a priest of Bahau origin, Yulius Aloysius Husin, had become the first interior Dayak member of East Kalimantan's DPRDGR. He soon joined Golkar, partly because of his association with the Kodam as a military chaplain, and in 1972 he was made East Kalimantan's representative in the MPR.[175] His steps were to be followed in 1977 by another Bahau-Benuaq politician, Dra. Emilia Lun Hadaitullah. Their appointments marked the emergence of the Bahau Dayak group, which resided in the interior of Kutai and had its center in Long Iram, as a significant political force. (In the 1955 election, they had not been represented because they did not yet have "modern" leaders of their own. While they mostly voted for the PNI, they were dominated by the Samarinda-Banjarese PNI leadership.) Their rise can in part be attributed to the political machinations of Kodam politicians who wanted to bring the Bahau Dayak group into the Golkar leadership in order to reduce the dominance of the Banjarese.

While the Catholic Bahau Dayaks joined Golkar, a very different Dayak group emerged in Bulungan *kabupaten*. Since the 1950s, there had been missionary activities by Protestant fundamentalist groups from America and Australia in the interior of Bulungan. After a brief halt imposed by Soeharjo, they continued their work in 1966. The alliance of

---

174 For a brief biography of Siel Stekanggen, see Biographical Appendix and **Buku MPR 1971**, p. 962.

175 For a brief biography of Yulius Aloysius Husin see Biographical Appendix and **Buku MPR 1971**, p. 961.

fundamentalist churches known as Kingmi (Kongres Injil Gereja Masehi Indonesia) with its headquarters in Bandung was an especially active missionary group after 1966.[176] The hub of Kingmi's religious activities is the *kecamatan* capital of Long Pujungan, while Tarakan has become the center for its political representatives. It was also in Tarakan that a strong Torajanese church developed to accommodate the religious needs of the Torajanese migrants.

Unlike the Bahau group, the Kayan-Kenyah Dayaks of Bulungan preferred to join the Protestant party, Parkindo (Indonesian Christian Party). In 1966, one of its leaders, Lentjang BA, was appointed a member of the BPH of Bulungan *kabupaten*. In the 1971 election, he was elected a member of Parliament (DPR) representing Parkindo. He was re-elected in 1977 as a candidate of the PDI and has been appointed secretary of the PDI faction in Parliament. He is thus the first Dayak leader from East Kalimantan to play a prominent role in national politics.[177]

The consolidation of Wahab Sjahranie's power was also facilitated by the weakening of the Kodam. Soekadijo's failure to obtain the governorship was in part caused by the resentment that had built up against the Kodam in Samarinda as a result of the events that had taken place during Soeharjo's time. Moreover, the Kodam had lacked an effective political leadership since Soekadijo's departure to Samarinda to become Acting Governor. The Pangdam, Mung Parhadimuljo, was uninterested in building up the political power of the Kodam, and there was no Chief of Staff capable of providing the leadership that the Kodam required. Not until the appointment in 1968 of Colonel Soeparno of the Brawijaya as the new Chief of Staff did the Kodam start to take political initiatives again. By that time, however, Wahab Sjahranie had already assured his dominance of Golkar.

Soeparno's arrival lifted the morale of the officers of the Kodam. A former secondary school teacher before joining the army during the Revolution, Soeparno had proved himself an able politician. Upon his

---

176 For the role of the Kingmi church, see *Laporan Survey Keadaan Kehidupan Beragama dan Aliran-Aliran Kepercayaan Masyarakat dikabupaten Berau dan Bulungan* (Samarinda: IAIN Sunan Ampel, 1977), pp. 16-42.

177 For a brief biography of Lentjang, see Biographical Appendix and *Buku MPR 1977*, pp. 692-93.

appointment as Chief of Staff, he took charge of political operations and brought Golkar its victory in the 1971 election. In 1970, he became the chairman of Golkar in East Kalimantan and used this position to try to stop the growing power of Wahab Sjahranie.[178]

However, Soeparno's efforts against Sjahranie were constrained by various factors. The first was the emergence of the police as an important player in provincial politics, due to the army leadership vacuum between 1965 and 1967. Wahab Sjahranie was quick to capitalize on this vacuum by giving the eager police the two bupatiships of Bulungan and Balikpapan. Two police majors of Banjarese origin were appointed Bupati, Asnawie Arbain for Bulungun and Zaenal Arifin for Balikpapan.[179]

Moreover, Soeparno was inhibited by the new Army Headquarters policy of limiting the tenure of the Regional Commander and of Kodam Chiefs of Staff. A Chief of Staff could now serve a maximum of four years in one Kodam, while the Pangdam had an even shorter tenure, between two and three years. This policy was aimed at preventing these officers from building power bases in their respective regions.

Furthermore, Army Headquarters made sure that the position of Pangdam of Mulawarman Kodam was rotated between the three important Javanese divisions, Brawijaya, Diponegoro, and Siliwangi.[180] Hence, during his four years as Chief of Staff, Soeparno had to serve three different Pangdam from three different divisions; namely, Brigadier General Mung Parhadimuljo (1965 to 1970), Brigadier General Soekertijo

---

178 For a brief biography of Colonel Soeparno, see Biographical Appendix and **Buku MPR 1977**, pp. 760-61.

179 Zaenal Arifin, a major of police was appointed mayor of Balikpapan by Wahab Sjahranie in 1970. However, he was unable to finish his tenure because he was accused of having been a member of the BPI (State Intelligence Bureau) prior to 1966. He was replaced by a fellow Banjarese police officer, Major Asnawie Arbain, who was then Bupati of Bulungan. The Bupatiship of Bulungan went to a Kodam officer, Lieutenant Colonel Soetadji, the former press officer of Soeharjo. It seems that the accusation against Zaenal Arifin originated at the Kodam Mulawarman which wanted to reduce the power of the police at the provincial level.

180 While Hartojo was a Diponegoro man, Soeharjo and Sumitro came from the Brawijaya division. Although he had served briefly in the Brawijaya, Mung Parhadimuljo was considered as having no special loyalty to any one particular division and was an RPKAD man. Soekertijo was a Brawijaya officer while Mantik was a Siliwangi man. The Pangdam after him, Brigadier Generals Sukotjo and Ery Supardjan, were both from Diponegoro. The next Pangdam, Brigadier General Rachwono, had spent most of his time in Diponegoro but was also a member of the Yogya military academy-generation which did not place much importance on the old Kodam divisions.

(1970-1971), and Brigadier General Mantik (1971-1973). Soeparno got strong support from his fellow Brawijaya officer, Soekertijo, but the latter's very brief tenure prevented any rebuilding of Brawijaya power in East Kalimantan comparable to the power Soeharjo had exercised.[181]

It was Wahab Sjahranie who profited most from the weakening of Kodam unity and its periodic lack of leadership. He himself was not only militarily senior to most of the Pangdam, let alone Chiefs of Staff, but his tenure as Governor was firmly set at five years. During his 10-year tenure as Governor (he was reappointed in 1972) Wahab Sjahranie dealt with five different Pangdam and five Chiefs of Staff.[182]

While the above factors played important roles in consolidating Sjahranie's power, his main initial advantage was his control over the timber concessions in East Kalimantan. At least prior to the centralization of timber licensing in 1970, Sjahranie was in a position to build a system of patronage based on his authority to assign timber concessions.

The economic potential of East Kalimantan's forests had been realized early on by Muis Hassan. In 1963 he had invited a team of Philippine businessmen to do a preliminary survey to assess the commercial feasibility of timber exploitation. But one month after they started their survey, Soeharjo ordered them out of East Kalimantan. A similar fate befell a group of Sabah businessmen. (Their interest in East Kalimantan timber can be explained by the shortage of timber reserves in the Philippines and Sabah by the middle of the 1960s.) While Muis Hassan could not overcome a political climate hostile to foreign timber concessions, he was able to reduce the ownership of timber reserves of the state-owned forest company, Perhutani (Perusahaan Hutan Negara Indonesia -- Indonesian State Forest Company). As early as 1959, the provincial government had asked for actual control over some of the timber areas in East Kalimantan then under Perhutani's control. In response to these appeals, the provincial

---

181 Soekertijo is a real Brawijaya officer, coming from the Lumayang area. He was appointed an Assistant for Logistics (Fourth Assistant) in 1971, but retired in 1975.

182 The average tenure in office of the Pangdam and Kasdam is about two years. During such a short tenure, they do not have the time to build their own power bases. Moreover, an appointment as Kasdam does not necessarily follow the Pangdam appointment, making it still more difficult for the Kodam to consolidate their power within the province. The post-1966 Kasdam have been: Colonel Soeparno (1968-1972), Colonel Soeroto (1972-1975), Colonel H.R.N. Pajouw (1975-1977), Colonel Moergito (1977-1978), Colonel Goenadi (1978-1979), and Colonel CZI Sarwono (1979-1981). See **Sejarah *Kodam Mulawarman***, p. 25.

Dinas Kehutanan (Forestry Service) was created to manage the timber areas outside the jurisdiction of Perhutani.[183]

Control over the timber areas was important not only in terms of the allocation of financial rights between the provincial and central governments, but also because of the vast size of East Kalimantan's forests. It was then estimated that the timber-producing area of East Kalimantan's forest was about 17.3 million hectares. It was considered the richest forest area in Indonesia because of its accessibility to river transportation, especially along the Mahakam and Kahayan rivers.

The conflict between the provincial and central government over concession rights reemerged in mid-1967 as foreigners were again allowed to exploit East Kalimantan's timber under Law 1/1967. Aside from the forest area already under Perhutani, the central government also demanded the ultimate right to give concessions to other areas. The provincial government considered the 3.7 million hectares under Perhutani already a vast zone. Moreover, since the central government had taken over all the oil royalties since 1950, the East Kalimantan government thought that it was only appropriate for it to benefit from local forest resources, through licenses, fees, and taxes. But the conflict between the provincial government of Wahab Sjahranie and the Directorate-General of Forestry (Ditjen Kehutanan) could not be legally resolved in the absence since 1956 of a law striking a new financial balance between the central and regional governments.[184]

Since political conditions immediately after the G-30-S Affair did not allow the central government to insist on a fully centralized policy, a formula was found to share the benefit of the exploitation of timber. The Governor was granted the power to give concessions up to 10,000 hectares, while the Bupati could give up to 5,000 hectares.

---

183 Perhutani was later changed into a state company for East and South Kalimantan, PT Inhutani II, under the directorship of a Javanese, Goenari. It controls about 3.2 million hectares of forest in East Kalimantan alone. The Dinas Kehutanan (Provincial Forestry Service) controls about 14 million hectares of forest, according to the provisions of the 1959 regulation which set up this new provincial forestry service. However, such control has been nullified by the power of Ditjen Kehutanan (Director General of Forestry) to grant HPH license.

184 UU number 32/1956 still provides the regulation framework for balancing the central government's financial claims against provincial claims. For a discussion of this balancing problem, see, for example, Raja Intan Joesoef, "Pengaruh Bantuan Keuangan Pusat Terhadap Pemerintahan Daerah" (MA thesis, Yogyakarta: Gajah Mada University, 1970), p. 245.

Any timber venture exploiting over 10,000 hectares had to obtain the permission of the Ditjen Kehutanan. These ventures, moreover, had to commission a survey by a recognized agency, sign a forestry agreement (FA), and accept certain replanting, environmental protection, and annual planning conditions in order to qualify for a concession permit.[185] Only then would the government give HPH (Hak Pengusahaan Hutan -- Forest Concession Rights) to applicants.

The concessions given by the Bupati and the Governor, on the other hand, required no such delicate procedures. Hence, various family-owned firms were established to cut the timber without using mechanical tools. Concessions as small as 100 hectares were doled out, sometimes to political favorites. People in the interior could get licenses from their *camat* and go to the forest to cut whatever they found. Most small firms and families used the traditional type of transport, the *banjirkap* (log-flood). The idea was to accumulate the timber up river and wait until the monsoon floods came, to carry the timber, free of charge, to the river mouths. At a time when the world price of timber was very good, the *banjirkap* type of venture attracted a lot of people. Its labor-intensive nature could absorb many workers, who came to East Kalimantan precisely for this reason. For the license holders, the start-up capital needed was relatively small. A concession of up to 5,000 hectares could be opened with about 200 million *rupiah*. Moreover, the license-holders could start with even less capital, provided they could pay the wages and minimum living expenses of their laborers, such as food and shelter. If they could time correctly the coming of the flood to a matter of days, they could further minimize production costs.

Hence, the *banjirkap* method greatly benefitted small firms, laborers, and the importers. The latter could bargain for sales terms better than those offered by the big companies which had long specialized in timber. Grants under 10,000 hectares also enabled the Governor, the Bupati and the *camat* to have personal shares in timber enterprises. The period between 1967 and 1970 was considered a happy and prosperous one

---

185 For a review of these licensing procedures, see M. J. Kasijanto, "Masalah Pertambangan Kayu," *Kompas*, August 31, 1978. See also, Ibrahimsjah Rachman, "Industri Perkayuan di Kaltim dan setumpuk Permasalahannya," ibid., June 27, 1979, and *Laporan Perkembangan Pengusahaan Hutan* (Jakarta: Ditjen Kehutanan, 1978), p. 12.

by most of the people of East Kalimantan who in one way or another benefitted from the *banjirkap* ventures.

On the other hand, bigger companies which had got HPH from the Ditjen Kehutanan, especially those with concessions ranging from 50,000 to 300,000 hectares in size were unhappy with the proliferation of *banjirkap* ventures. It proved difficult for them to get cheap labor, because workers preferred to work for the *banjirkap* ventures or for small firms where the salaries were better. In fact, laborers who saved enough money could even become shareholders of these small ventures themselves.

But the biggest companies, with concessions of 300,000 hectares on up, could depend on their modern equipment and low labor costs to benefit fully from their huge concessions. They were not seriously threatened by the small firms, due to their economies of scale. Although they did face some difficulties in finding cheap workers, they could import workers directly from Java and South Sulawesi.

However, the competitive prices of the *banjirkap* ventures and small firms were an annoyance even to the biggest companies. These large companies, which were mostly multinationals, had experience in exploiting timber in Sabah, South Korea, the Philippines, and Taiwan. They did not like the idea that small firms and individuals could determine the price of timber at their expense. They wanted to be able to determine timber markets, since in the end these prices would determine their profits.

These large foreign companies were able to find various powerful people within the central government in Jakarta that worried also about the impact of the *banjirkap* and small ventures. Some people at the Ditjen Kehutanan worried about the fact that timber exploitation in East Kalimantan had not been accompanied by any timber processing efforts. The export-oriented nature of forest exploitation was considered a waste of natural resources. Hence, they saw the need to force the timber ventures to add an industrial phase to their activities. To this end, these bureaucrats believed that the timber companies should be required to establish plywood and other type of industries in order to obtain a license to operate. This policy, it was argued, would protect Indonesia from becoming another Sabah or Mindanao, areas which the foreign companies simply left after having nearly exhausted their timber reserves. Others were concerned with the need to finance governmental projects by the exploitation of timber and, especially, to increase the share of the central government. If East Kalimantan was to be allowed to take for itself most of the concession rights, then other regions could well demand the same thing. Although the *banjirkap* operations and small firms provided the central government with a large amount of revenue, central government bureaucrats were certain that the centralization of the licensing process would maximize the central government's revenue intake. Moreover, there were some bureaucrats and politicians in Jakarta who feared that the exploitation of timber was being used to accumulate substantial economic power outside of the central government's control. Still, many other central government officers were more than attracted by the possibility that the centralization of the HPH granting process would allow them to get funds easily for any purpose they had in mind. This was particularly true for the many *yayasan* (foundations) of the armed forces, which hoped to use the funds generated from the timber concessions to pay for the welfare of the troops in ways not covered by the annual budget.

Prior to the taking over of all HPH by the Ditjen Kehutanan, there were only a few foreign companies with timber concessions. The biggest of all was Kayan River Timber Products (KRTP), a Philippine subsidiary of an American company. It had about 1.2 million hectares along the Kayan River in Bulungan. The KRTP was a typical pre-1970 company in that it was wholly foreign-owned.

The actual centralization of HPH procedures was enacted in 1970 by Presidential decree, the Keppres No. 20/1970. The level at which the decision was made shows that the delicate allocational issues raised by the concession rights centralization question had to be taken at the very top. The Decree was a major victory for the Director General of Forestry, Soedjarwo,[186] who all along had argued for the centralization of HPH

---

186 Soedjarwo's power came partly from the association of his wife with the Mangkunegaran family (**trah**) to which the First Lady, Mrs. Tien Suharto, also belongs. Aside from that, Soedjarwo also has led the Javanese mysticism group, Paguyuban Ngesti Tunggal (Pangestu), which has a strong following among *priyayi* officials. Soedjarwo became the longest serving high official from the Guided Democracy period to stay on during the New Order. He remained in office from 1964 to 1988. In the 1983 Cabinet reshuffle, he was promoted from Director General to lead his own Ministry of Forestry as a minister. In 1988 he was replaced as forestry minister by Hasjrul Harahap, but only after he completed the building of a huge forestry complex in Jakarta, Manggala Wana Bhakti, which was financed totally by the timber companies.

allocations, and later promoted the 1982 Decree which banned the export of logs in order to promote the Indonesian plywood industry.[187]

The new regulation stipulated that the minimum size of a timber concession was to be 50,000 hectares. The Governor and the Bupati were not allowed to make any concessions, although a limited number of small concessions of 100 hectares were permitted. Medium-sized ventures (10,000 hectares or so) had to merge with other enterprises to achieve the minimum of 50,000 hectares. Moreover, the labor-intensive cutting of timber was prohibited on the basis that such practices could make replanting difficult. Timber exploitation now had to be done by mechanical tools.

This policy clearly benefitted the large companies which had strong connections in Jakarta and the ability to work out joint-venture agreements with foreigners. Lack of capital prevented the local companies, even those with 10,000 hectare licenses, to continue operations without the addition of new funds. Small firms and individual ventures began going bankrupt.[188]

A further effect of the new policy was to create massive unemployment among the unskilled laborers of the *banjirkap* type operations as well as an increased presence of skilled foreign workers (mostly Malaysians and Filipinos), as shown in Table 6.

The policy mainly benefitted those people in Jakarta who became "absentee concession holders" by getting HPH licenses from the Ditjen Kehutanan and renting them out to foreign operators. As "absentee concession holders," they received fees of between US$ 5 to US$ 10 per cubic meter of logs exported. Moreover, this "absentee HPH" system largely resulted in the uncontrolled exploitation of Kalimantan's timber.

---

187 The devastating effect of the *banjirkap* was mostly caused by Indonesia's lack of log-carrier transportation to the importing countries. Since the log-carrier facilities were monopolized by big companies, it seems that they deliberately planned the *banjirkap* catastrophe in order to encourage the Indonesian government to centralize the HPH-granting process in Indonesia. Moreover, since 1970, the big timber companies have created their own cartel, Majelis Perkayuan Indonesia (Indonesian Timber Council) which has determined the quotas of exports each year. Nevertheless, the government has decisive power in terms of the limits it can impose on the number of logs to be exported in order to induce the timber companies to undertake investments in timber processing facilities and to protect Indonesia's forest reserves.

188 See Kasijanto, "Masalah," in **Kompas**. See also, Sjafril Manan, "Manajemen Hutan Tropika Basah: Tantangan Bagi Rimbawan Indonesia," in **Kompas**, March 1, 1980 (originally a commencement day speech at the Bogor Agricultural Institute).

The adverse environmental consequences of this kind of exploitation were so severe that it was feared that East Kalimantan would soon exhibit the kinds of deforestation problems that Mindanao and Sabah had recently experienced.

Because of their close relations with the politically well-connected holders of the HPH in Jakarta, the foreign operators were encouraged to disregard the Ditjen Kehutanan's regulations. Not only did they not follow the regulations regarding the size of trees to be cut, the Tebang Pilih Indonesia (Indonesian Selection on Cutting), but most did not even bother to give their annual plans (Rencana Kerja Tahunan-RKT) to the Ditjen Kehutanan. Only 21 percent of the 92 HPHs which started to operate in East Kalimantan after September 1970 started to do the reforestation required by the HPH rules. Controlling about 10.2 million hectares of East Kalimantan's total of 17.3 million hectares of timber areas, they cut 1.9 million hectares and replanted only 7,121 hectares (0.4 percent). As a direct consequence, almost 2 million hectares of East Kalimantan forest became "bald land" (*tanah gundul*), susceptible to forest fires at any time. Hence, the deforestation that took place in the years between 1967 and 1980 of large-scale forest exploitation dwarfs the mere 100,000 hectares of "bald land" left by the practices of local shifting cultivators who have been blamed so much in recent years for the region's deforestation problems.[189]

The damage done to East Kalimantan's forest by the mechanization of timber exploitation increasingly concerned Indonesian forest experts. It was suggested that the HPH holders should pay US$ 4 per cubic meter of logs harvested to fund a replanting budget. Moreover, it was suggested that HPH holders should be punished for their disregard of regulations, including such regulatory violations as taking logs from corridors outside their agreement areas and cutting timber in protected forest areas.[190] However, in answering these complaints, the Ditjen Kehutanan was quick to point out that Indonesia's laws are poorly crafted to deal with these

---

189 See a report in *Kompas*, February 11, 1980, p. 1.
190 Ibid., February 12, 1980. It was reported that companies have cut a 50 meters wide corridor in violation of government regulations and that about 200,000 hectares of protected forest in Bontang, Kutai were exploited without government consent.

Table 6. The changes in employment in timber concessions between
1969 and 1975

| Years | Mechanical | | | % of | | % of | |
	Indonesians	Foreigners	Total	Total	Banjirkap	Total	Total
1969/1970	1,901	977	2,878	19	12,500	81	15,375
1970/1971	3,216	3,511	4,727	16	25,000	84	29,729
1971/1972	6,944	2,511	9,495	32	20,000	68	29,495
1972/1973	8,185	3,022	11,027	69	5,000	31	16,207
1973/1974	12,708	3,796	16,504	100	-	-	6,504
1974/1975	13,547	2,178	15,725	100	-	-	15,725

Source: *Kalimantan Timur dalam Repelita I dan II* (Samarinda: Bappeda Kalimantan Timur, 1978), p. 132.

forest exploitation abuses.[191] In addition, the Ditjen Kehutanan also lacked the personnel necessary to supervise the exploitation, not to mention the necessary political support and clout to enforce a punishment scheme against timber operators who had obtained important political backing from Jakarta's power cliques. The most visible result of this negligent and greedy form of forest exploitation was the terrible fire of 1983 which destroyed about 3 million hectares of East Kalimantan's forests.

At the same time, the mechanization of timber exploitation considerably increased both timber production levels and government foreign exchange revenue levels. Tables 7 and 8 show Indonesia's overall export figures and East Kalimantan's share in the 1970s. The increased activity of the HPH holders and timber exploitation business after 1970 meant that East Kalimantan was producing between 30 and 40 percent of the nation's exports as well as leading the timber producing provinces in exports. However, if production for domestic consumption is taken into account, East Kalimantan was producing about two thirds of the total national timber supply.[192]

---

191 A speech by Dirjen Kehutanan, Soedjarwo, in *Kompas*, May 20, 1980. See also Manan, "Manajemen," and *Kompas*, February 11, 1980 in which it was stated that Indonesia does not have a law to punish the violators of HPH licenses.
192 See *Kalimantan Timur Dalam Repelita I dan II* (Samarinda: Bappeda Kalimantan Timur,

The new policy also adjusted the allocation of log revenues to the benefit of the central government. Various fees and taxes were designed to give more revenues to Jakarta. Hence, the shifting of profit from the small firms with provincial bases to the large companies with headquarters in Jakarta was also accompanied by a greater flow of revenues to the central government than to the provincial government.

The 1970 regulation describes ten types of fees and taxes to be taken from timber production and its beneficiaries.[193] Of these taxes and fees, the most profitable and important ones were taken by the central government, including the License Fee (IHPH-Iuran Hak Pengusahaan Hutan) and the Additional Forest Royalty (IHHT-Iuran Hasil Hutan Tambahan). Less profitable taxes were given to the provincial government, namely the Forest Product Royalty (IHH-Iuran Hasil Hutan) and Forestry Local Government Tax (Ipeda-Iuran Pembangunan Daerah).

Although the provincial and *kabupaten* governments have earned a smaller share of the timber exploitation profits since the end of the 1970s, they have still profited immensely from the timber business. Among the taxes that are taken by the local governments are the timber retribution and logs pond retribution taxes. The *kabupaten* governments also have their own state-run timber exploitation companies (*perusahaan daerah*), while the village heads and *camat* benefit from the timber taxes given to them to administer.[194] According to estimates of East Kalimantan's Bappeda, about 40 percent of the provincial budget in the late 1970s came from the fees and taxes on timber exploitation.

1978), p. 131. Aside from East Kalimantan, the major timber producers have been Riau, South Sumatra, South Kalimantan, Central Kalimantan, West Kalimantan, Central Sulawesi, and Maluku. For a listing of timber exporters, see *Petunjuk Eksportir Hasil Hutan Indonesia, 1973-1978* (Jakarta: Ditjen Kehutanan, 1979), annual publication, p. 15.

193 See Abdul Rachman Fomia, "Management Eksploitasi Hutan dan Pengaruhnya Atas Potensi Pengembangan Daerah" (MA thesis, Jakarta: Institut Ilmu Pemerintahan, 1974), pp. 52-65. Also *Kalimantan Repelita I dan II*, p. 49.

194 The Kutai *kabupaten* has its own company. In Tarakan, each cooperative unit of the armed forces has its own concession, working jointly with a foreign company. See *Monografi*, p. 5. The Korpri, government employee organization, also has its own concession, PT Praja Mukti, working with "Limbang Timber Coy" from Malaysia. See Fomia, "Management," p. 38.

Table 7. Indonesia's timber exports between 1971 and 1978

Year	Volume (in 1,000 m³)	Value (in US$ 1.000)
1971	10,761	168.63
1972	13,891	230.34
1973	19,433	583.35
1974	18,082	725.55
1975	13,921	499.97
1976	18,521	781.75
1977	19,992	951.27
1978	19,202	939.66

Source: **Laporan Dirjen 1979** (Jakarta: Ditjen Kehutanan, 1979) lampiran VI.

Table 8. Log exports from East Kalimantan 1970-1975

Year	Volume (in 1,000 m³)	Value (in US$ 1,000)
1970	2,665	not available
1971	4,548	71.66
1972	4,601	79.69
1973	6,306	123.17
1974	7,623	316.88
1975	6,929	307.43

Source: **Kalimantan Timur Dalam Repelita I and II** (Samarinda: Buppeda Kalimantan Timur, 1978), p. 133.

Table 9 shows the central government's share of East Kalimantan's timber exploitation profits between 1969 and 1978.

The shifting of economic power from the provincial-based firms and officials to the central government's agencies and Jakarta-based companies undercut Wahab Sjaranie's political patronage system. Although the provincial-based companies still could merge, or work as agents of the larger companies in Jakarta, most of the profits from timber exploitation were now funneled to Jakarta or other areas outside East Kalimantan itself.

So the Governor's loss of decision-making power to the central government in terms of the distribution of timber licenses meant that the Governor could no longer use the timber concessions as political tender. Up to 1970, many local operators worked in the timber business, managing small concessions, ranging from 100 hectares to 10,000 hectares. They were given the licenses by the Governor or Bupati and employed the migrants that came from Java, South Kalimantan, and South Sulawesi.

The effect of the policy was felt particularly strongly among the Banjarese businessmen in Balikpapan and Samarinda. They controlled the provincial and *kabupaten* bureaucracies through their fellow Banjarese, who in turn rewarded them with timber licenses. These businessmen owned mostly small and middle-sized ventures with capital assets of up to 100 million rupiahs. However, they employed many people in labor-intensive types of jobs.

The new policy resulted in the concentration of concessions in the hands of individuals who were well connected to the central government. There were two types of concession holders. First, there were the *yayasan* that were linked to the various power cliques in Jakarta, and mostly operated directly in East Kalimantan. In many cases, these foundations worked closely with foreign companies which had earlier amassed experience in the timber business elsewhere. The second group of holders consisted of individuals who had been given a license but did not have either the capital or the experience to participate in the timber business. In most cases, these individuals subcontracted their license to other companies, mostly from the Philippines and Malaysia.

The main losers in this new decision-making arrangement were the bureaucrats in Samarinda and the provincial businessmen, who had depended on the provincial government to reap the financial rewards of the timber business. Most of these businessmen were Banjarese and resided either in Samarinda or Balikpapan. The provincial bureaucrats not only lost the power to grant licenses, but also the chance of funding their local bid for political power through the timber concessions.

Because the economic and political stakes involved were so high, the central government decided to exercise a strong grip on the political process in East Kalimantan to prevent any threat to its interests. Since the post-Soeharjo politics of East Kalimantan were dominated by various Banjarese groups (i.e., the Samarinda-based PNI; the *pejuang* of Balikpapan and Samarinda, and more recently, the groups around Wahab Sjahranie), the central government had been particularly concerned with reducing the power of the Banjarese leadership.

It should be noted that, despite his close association with many Banjarese groups such as the PSI group and the *pejuang*, Wahab Sjahranie was still an army officer whose loyalty had always been to the national cause and central government. Sjahranie's leadership, however, was acceptable to many Banjarese groups who saw in his leadership a solution to the growing presence of the Javanese in East Kalimantan. Nevertheless under the Kodam leadership of Pangdam Soekertijo and Kasdam

Table 9. The income of the East Kalimantan provincial government and the central government from timber, 1969/1970 to 1977/1978[a]

Year	Income of *Pemda*	Income of *Pusat*
	(both in million of rupiah)	
1969/1970	1,847.2	257.2
1970/1971	1,805.3	516.8
1971/1972	2,493.8	1,342.4
1972/1973	3,009.4	5,110.5
1973/1974	4,739.6	6,700.1
1974/1975	3,663.5	5,431.8
1975/1976	3,216.4	4,993.0
1976/1977	5,923.6	7,150.4
1977/1978	8,333.1	8,200.6

Source: **Perkembangan Reboisasi dan Penghijauan di Kalimantan Timur** (Samarinda: Bappeda Kalimantan Timur, 1979), p. 15.

[a] Not including foreign exchange, which is mostly taken by the Center and only returned to *daerah* in terms of the local currency subsidy.

Soeparno, competition increased between the Javanese and Banjarese over the distribution of positions and other political benefits provided by Golkar's 1971 election victory.

The solid victory of the Islamic parties (later to be merged into a single party, PPP) in the Balikpapan and Samarinda areas, in a way replaced the PNI's power base in the Banjarese community. While a few of the Banjarese were still loyal and voted for the PNI, most Banjarese in these two cities realized that in their competition with the Javanese, the Islamic parties were the answer. Some other Banjarese, however, especially the former PNI bureaucrats in Samarinda and Kutai, voted for Golkar. (See Tables 10 and 11 for the election results in 1971 and 1977.)

The political climate prevalent during the 1971 election was heavily influenced by the central government's takeover of timber exploitation in East Kalimantan. Many Banjarese felt threatened by the central government, and through it, by the Javanese in East Kalimantan province. Hence, the Islamic party in the 1970s was seen as the party of the Banjarese, as the PNI had been in the 1950s and 1960s. Within the PDI itself (which emerged in 1972 from the forced merger of all non-Islamic parties), the Samarinda-based PNI was losing ground to the increasingly powerful Kenyah-Kayan-based Parkindo. Old top leaders of the PNI, such as Muis Hassan and Inche Abdul Muis, had moved to Jakarta, while provincial leaders, such as Azis Samad and Sjachrumsjah Idris, had kept a low profile, due to the strong anti-PNI campaign in the late 1960s.

The effect of this political configuration was to make Wahab Sjahranie the new leader of the Samarinda group, and of the Banjarese, against an increasingly politically consolidated Kodam, led mostly by Javanese

Table 10. The results of the 1971 election

	Kabupaten	Golkar	PPP	PDI
1.	Samarinda	30,317	25,780	4,518
2.	Balikpapan	34,613	17,726	4,606
3.	Kutai	61,204	34,249	22,370
4.	Berau	10,217	4,316	474
5.	Bulungan	28,259	7,229	15,118

6.	Pasir	15,518	9,767	2,599
	Total East Kalimantan	180,128	99,067	49,685

Source: Panitia Pemilihan Indonesia, Lembaga Pemilihan Umum.

Table 11. The results of the 1977 election

	Kabupaten	Golkar	PPP	PDI
1.	Samarinda	39,282	41,730	6,196
2.	Balikpapan	36,091	51,502	9,477
3.	Kutai	81,126	45,843	12,902
4.	Berau	13,572	5,399	922
5.	Bulungan	49,076	9,740	4,088
6.	Pasir	32,982	7,832	811
	Total: East Kalimantan	252,129	162,046	34,396

Source: Lembaga Pemilihan Umum.

officers. This configuration also worked to the advantage of Kutai aristocrats such as AR Padmo who was appointed a member of the MPR representing East Kalimantan. Neither Wahab Sjahranie nor the Kodam leadership wanted to exclude the Kutai aristocracy from provincial politics and government. The former believed that the Kutai aristocrats could be counted on as supporters in dealing with the Kodam, while the latter realized that the Kutai and other indigenous groups, such as the Bahau, could be used to reduce the power of the Banjarese.

At the same time, local Javanese profited from the rivalry between the Kodam leadership and Sjahranie. While nearly 20 percent of the province's population was Javanese, they were behind the Banjarese economically. They mostly worked in the oil sector as laborers and in the timber business, also as workers. The establishment of Skarda (Staf Kekaryaan Daerah -- Regional Functional Staff) assured the Javanese of Kodam institutional support in protecting their local interests.[195] Important positions within the Skarda were held mainly by Javanese officers who maintained close contact with the labor leaders in the oil sector and the businessmen from the timber sector, who were mostly non-Banjarese. From 1974 onward, the Kodam, led by the Kaskarda (Kepala Staf Skarda) took many new initiatives in dealing with provincial problems. The person who headed these initiatives was a Brawijaya officer, Colonel Jhonet Hutomo. In 1974, the Chairmanship of the DPRD was taken over by a fellow Brawijaya officer, Colonel Sukotjo SM, who had once been the Kodim of Kutai during the Soeharjo era. In that year, another Brawijaya officer from the Soeharjo era, Lieutenant Colonel Soetadji, was appointed as Bupati of Bulungan.[196]

Meanwhile, the Kodam had been able to reduce the power of the police, which had grown to fill the power vacuum in Balikpapan in the late 1960s. The MPR members from East Kalimantan's police were reduced from two in the 1971 elections to none in the 1977 election, excluding the provincial chief of police.[197] However, after 1973, the Pangdam always came from the Diponegoro division, preventing the full consolidation of Brawijaya power. While they differed on who should lead the Kodam, these officers were all determined to give a larger share of power to the non-Banjarese in East Kalimantan. In short, the presence of the Kodam helped to guarantee a larger share of power to the non-Banjarese and to

---

195 The Skarda office is headed by the Fifth Assistant to the Pangdam and responsible to the Skarwil (Staf Kekaryaan Wilayah) at the Kowilhan (Defense Regional Command) level. However, because the officers in the Skarda office change regularly, the real power at the Kodam level lies in the highest ranking officer who has stayed longest in the job relating to functional affairs. In East Kalimantan, officers such as Colonel Soetadji and Colonel Sukotjo could well brief the new Skarda who would not know much about the political situation of the province.

196 Despite rumors to the contrary, Colonel Soetadji was reappointed as Bupati of Bulungan, an office in which he has served since 1974. Prior to that, he was the Head of the Social Political Bureau of the Governor's Office and was Soeharjo's press officer during the latter's service as Pangdam. He is one of a few officers of Brawijaya origin who still retains power in East Kalimantan. His reappointment as Bupati occurred in June 1980.

197 In 1971, two police officers represented the armed forces in the MPR. They were the Provincial Police Chief (Kadapol), Brigadier General Drs. Sumardhi, and Lieutenant Colonel Drs. Jourdanus Nitidibrata. The latter is a Bantenese officer who had resided in East Kalimantan since 1962. However, more recently the nature of his career advancement required him to move outside of East Kalimantan. At the time of his appointment, he was the provincial Secretary of Golkar. See *Buku MPR 1971*, pp. 1112 and 1071. In the 1977 election neither the Kadapol Brigadier General Drs. R. Hardiman nor other police officers were appointed as members of MPR.

defend the interests of the central government in timber exploitation.

Nevertheless, his seniority and his handling of the short tenure of the Pangdams did enable Wahab Sjahranie to gain the upper hand in the provincial branch of Golkar. He brought his old acquaintance from Banjarmasin, Colonel RM Parwono, in to head Golkar after Colonel Soeparno left. The extent of Sjahranie's success is reflected by the composition of the membership of the DPR and MPR in the 1977 election, where he was able to put his wife in as a member of the DPR.[198]

Despite this success, time was running out for Wahab Sjahranie, and especially for the Banjarese of East Kalimantan. The increasing presence of the Javanese, the emergence of local leaders from various Dayak groups, and the increasing association of the Banjarese with the Islamic party all worked against him. But the most decisive factor, it seems, was the increasing economic stakes of various power groups in Jakarta in the timber and other economic resources of East Kalimantan.

After the financial failure of the KRTP company in Bulungan-Berau in the early 1970s, three companies dominated the leadership of the timber exploitation business in East Kalimantan. The first was an Army-*yayasan* related company, ITCI (International Timber Corporation Indonesia), which works jointly with the American company Weyerhauser and has about 1 million hectares of concessions in the Balikpapan and Kutai areas. The ITCI was also under contract to exploit forest concessions with the Army-related company, PT Tri Usaha Bhakti, and hence, had indirect institutional ties with the Kodam.[199]

Another company is related to Bob Hasan, a *peranakan* Chinese businessman with army ties in Jakarta, who heads the Georgia Pacific Indonesia Company (PT GPI) and holds an area of more than 600,000 hectares in the Upper Mahakam. Hasan also owns plywood plants and other forest-related businesses numbering, he acknowledges, "between 20 and 30 companies." By 1988, he had become chairman of four out of the five federations of forest-related associations. In June of that year he

---

198 For a brief biography of Mrs. Adjang Ratminie Sjahranie see Biographical Appendix and **Buku MPR 1977**, p. 650.

199 The PT ITCI (International Timber Corporation Indonesia) has about 500,000 hectares of concession lands in the Kutai and Balikpapan areas. According to reports, the company did not start any replanting process as required by its concession agreement. See Laurens Samsoeri, "PT ITCI dan PT GPI Belum melakukan peremajaan hutan," in **Sinar Harapan**, June 28, 1979.

was also elected chairman of the umbrella organization for all the forest-related associations, the Indonesian Forest Council (Majelis Perkayuan Indonesia).[200]

The third company is led by another *peranakan* Chinese, Jos Sutomo, who heads the Sumber Mas Group with plywood plants in Gresik, East Java, and in Samarinda. Like Bob Hasan, Jos Sutomo has converted to Islam and has made a pilgrimage to Mecca with his own private plane. In 1980, Jos Sutomo had bought up the huge timber concession previously owned by the KRTP in the Bulungan area, adding to his previously obtained concession holding in Kutai. However, in the early 1980s he did not have ties with any of Jakarta's powerful political groups. He was prosecuted in 1983 and was sentenced to two years in prison for tax evasion and tax fraud. Along with his convicted brother, Ava Sutomo, Jos Sutomo made an appeal to the High Court and obtained a reduced sentence. He then made another appeal to the Supreme Court, which ordered his release in 1988.

In 1988 Jos Sutomo also re-entered the timber business arena as a significant player. This has largely been due to the ties he has been able to forge with Jakarta's powerful military groups. By 1988, he had sold 25 percent of his shares to the Army-*yayasan* company, PT Tri Usaha Bhakti. Moreover, the general manager of the Sumber Mas Group in 1988 was retired Colonel Soekotjo SM, the former chairman of the East Kalimantan provincial DPRD. At the same time, Jos Sutomo is also quite popular within the Islamic Banjarese community, in large part because of his donations for Islamic *dakwah* activities.[201] Thus he has forged ties with Jakarta's power groups while maintaining his popularity among the local groups in East Kalimantan.

From the above discussions, it can be seen that none of the three largest timber companies has any genuinely strong ties to the indigenous

---

200 For information on Mohammad (Bob) Hasan, see Biographical Appendix and *Tempo*, September 28, 1985, pp. 64-68. For information on the total number of Bob Hasan's companies, see *Tempo*, September 28, 1985, pp. 64-68.

201 According to prominent Samarinda Islamic leader Drs. Hamri Has, Sutomo contributed 300 million *rupiah* annually to various Islamic groups in East Kalimantan, including the Majelis Ulama. (Interviews with AR Sayid Gasjim Baraqbah and Drs. Hamri Has, June 20 and 24, 1979, respectively. Both Sayid Gasjim and Drs. Hamri Has are religious advisors to Jos Sutomo. Sayid Gasjim has even accompanied Jos Sutomo to Mecca. While in prison in Samarinda, Jos Sutomo built a tennis court in the prison complex.

people of East Kalimantan in terms of capital, ownership, or directorship. The former Sultan, Parikesit, sold his land in the Bengalon area to PT Porodisa, which is headed by the chairman of the Bouraq group, J. A. Sumendap, a prominent businessman of Talaud (North Sulawesi) origin. PT Porodisa holds about 300,000 hectares of concessionary land. When Sultan Parikesit complained to President Suharto about his fate as a former ruler without a forest concession to live from, he was indemnified by the government. Most of the timber companies are owned by members of Jakarta's powerful political groups who have no connections to the East Kalimantan populace. The only exception to this ownership pattern is the company led by the son of a Kutai aristocrat, PT Kutai Timber Indonesia. The company is directed by Aji Rustam Effendie, a son of AR Djokoprawiro, who also owns the largest hotel in Balikpapan, the Hotel Bina Kutai.

With all these regulatory changes, the Banjarese traders and officials were the hardest hit, because they could not compete with the *peranakan* Chinese businessmen who had ties with Jakarta's power groups as well as foreign connections. A few Kutai aristocrats like Aji Rustam Effendie were able to continue to benefit financially from the timber concessions. These aristocrats, however, are unable to use their concession holdings for political purposes due to the size of their companies and their dependence on foreign capital. Practical financial considerations had made it impossible for the aristocrats to compete with major timber businessmen such as Bob Hasan and Jos Sutomo.

The mechanization of timber exploitation has also brought businessmen with strong influence in national politics into East Kalimantan's political power equation. Moreover, it has brought various power groups, such as the army as a whole, the Kodam, and other groups close to Jakarta's power brokers, into the vortex of East Kalimantan's provincial politics. In such a climate, the Banjarese of East Kalimantan soon lost some of the power which they had maintained over the previous twenty years. Not only was Wahab Sjahranie unable to defend Banjarese interests against the demands of the central government and the Javanese, but he had to leave the governorship in 1978, after having served as Governor for eleven years.

The main candidate for the governorship in 1978 was none other than the then Pangdam, Brigadier General Ery Supardjan, a Diponegoro officer who was a close associate of many high officers from that division, including General Surono, then Vice Commander in Chief of the Armed Forces.[202] The efforts by the Samarinda Banjarese to enlist fellow Banjarese elsewhere as gubernatorial candidates proved to be a failure. Two officers were put forth as candidates by the Samarinda Banjarese, namely, the then Bupati of Kotabaru, South Kalimantan, Colonel Gusti Sjamsir Alam, and the director of the Army's Intelligence School in Bogor, Colonel Abdulmadjid. The Brawijaya group, on the other hand, supported the candidacy of Colonel Soeparno, then the mayor of Surabaya.[203] These candidates, however, were unable to compete with Ery Supardjan who was appointed by President Suharto to replace Wahab Sjahranie.

The appointment of Ery Supardjan marked the beginning of the decline of the Samarinda-Banjarese in East Kalimantan's political power structure. The new Governor appointed former bureaucratic cadres of the PNI as his main assistants while at the same time introducing Javanese bureaucrats into the provincial bureaucracy. He also reduced the power of the Banjarese by replacing many Bupati of Banjarese origins with Kutais, albeit of lower aristocratic backgrounds.[204]

---

202 For a brief biography of Brigadier Soepardjan, see Biographical Appendix and *Sinar Harapan*, June 19, 1978 and *Buku MPR 1977*, p. 724.

203 Colonel Soeparno may have lost the mayorship of Surabaya because of the difficulty he was having with the Governor. His successor was a Brawijaya officer of Malang origin, Lieutenant Colonel Muhadji Widjaya. Thus, the Brawijaya really did not have a strong candidate for the governorship of East Kalimantan in 1978. However, they tried to catch up in 1980 by proposing their officer, Brigadier General Mistar Tjokrokusumo, as a candidate for the governorship of South Kalimantan. Mistar had also been a former Pangdam there.

204 At the height of his power, in 1973, Governor Wahab Sjahranie was aided by the following Bupati of Banjarese origins:

Kutai	Drs. Achmad Dahlan
Bulungan	Major (Police) Asnawie Arbain
Berau	Masdar John BA
Pasir	Saleh Nafsi SH
Samarinda	Mohammad Kadrie Uning
Balikpapan	Major (Police) Zaenal Arifin

In contrast, Ery Soepardjan's appointments reduced the representation of the Banjarese leadership within the office of Bupati:

	Name	Ethnicity
Bupati of Kutai	Drs. Awang Faisal	Kutainese

On becoming Governor, Ery Supardjan had to face competition from the Kodam under the leadership of the then Pangdam, Brigadier General Rachwono. However, there were limits to the kinds of demands the Kodam could make, conditioned by the presence of many companies with Jakarta ties, the increasing Javanese population, and the emergence of indigenous groups, particularly the Dayak communities. Moreover, like Wahab Sjahranie before him, Ery Supardjan could take advantage of Rachwono's short tenure as Pangdam. Supardjan also strengthened his position within the Kodam group by appointing mayors and Bupati of Kodam origin. So, for example, when Mayor Asnawie Arbain of Balikpapan finished his term, Ery Supardjan chose the Kodim commander of Samarinda, Lieutenant Colonel Sjarifuddin Jus of Malay-Medan origin, as the new mayor. This mayoral appointment also reflected the emergence of the new generation of AMN-Akekad graduates as Bupati, mayors, Vice Governors, and Governors not only in East Kalimantan, but all over Indonesia.[205]

East Kalimantan's political map in the late 1970s and early 1980s, was considerably different from that of the early 1950s. The PNI's Samarinda-based Banjarese had fallen from power. Now they could not even get a single seat in the DPR. Their leader, Sjahrumsjah Idris, was only elected a member of the DPRD in the 1977 election. Within the Banjarese community, two new groups have emerged and taken over the political leadership of the community. The first group is the rising PPP (United Development Party). Since the 1971 election the six East Kalimantan DPR members have included two members of the PPP. This

Bupati of Berau	Masdar John BA (to be replaced soon)	Chinese/Banjarese
Bupati of Bulungan	Colonel Soetadji	Javanese
Bupati of Pasir	Drs. Awang Badaranie	Kutainese
Mayor of Samarinda	Drs. Anang Hasjim	Banjarese
Mayor of Balikpapan	Asnawie Arbain	Banjarese
Sekwilda Province	Mohammad Ardans SH	Banjarese

205 The first Governor to emerge from the AMN-ATEKAD group of graduates was C. J. Rantung in North Sulawesi. By July 1988, other AMN graduates also became Governors, namely Pardjoko in West Kalimantan; Raja Inal Siregar in North Sumatra; Pudjanto Pranjoto in Lampung. Many young officers have also become Vice Governors, most of them with the rank of Colonel: I Dewa Oka in Bali; Zainal Palaguna in South Sulawesi; Teuku Djohan in Aceh; Suryatna in West Java; Victor Phaing in Central Kalimantan; Brigadier General Basofi Sudirman in Greater Jakarta. The mayor of Bandung, Colonel Ateng Wahyudi, as well as many other mayors and Bupati are also AMN graduates.

Islamic party has been led mostly by *sarjana* of Islamic background such as Djaffar Siddik, a member of the DPR in Jakarta. The new religious self-consciousness among the Banjarese Islamic communities in Samarinda and Balikpapan has partly been caused by the threat that the Banjarese Islamic communities have increasingly come to feel from the growing presence of *abangan* Javanese in the region and from Christian missionary activities. Some Banjarese officials such as Mayor Asnawie Arbain of Balikpapan and Bupati Achmad Dahlan of Kutai have even founded *pesantren* schools in an effort to protect the religious identity and integrity of the Banjarese Islamic communities.

The second group of Banjarese consists of the young generation of Banjarese that by the late 1970s were cooperating closely with the central government through their work in the bureaucracy and Golkar. The leader of this bureaucratic group has been Mohammad Ardans who became Sekwilda in 1979 and then Vice Governor in 1985. In June 1988, Mohammad Ardans was appointed as the new Governor of East Kalimantan, replacing the sick Governor, retired Colonel Suwandi.[206] The appointment of Ardans as Governor was made possible through the support provided by the newly created all-Kalimantan Pangdam Tanjungpura, who happens to be a Banjarese officer of South Kalimantan origin, Major General Zein Maulani.[207] Many of the younger generation Banjarese have by now climbed up Golkar's political ladder at the *kabupaten*

---

206 Colonel Suwandi had two terms as Bupati of Lumajang, East Java, before he was appointed in 1983 to replace Ery Supardjan, who died shortly after leaving the office of Governor. Although he came from the Brawijaya division, Suwandi did not have experience with the Kodam in Balikpapan nor his own power base elsewhere in East Kalimantan. Hence, he did not change much of the legacy of Ery Supardjan. In 1986, he had a stroke and became incapacitated, prompting the central government to appoint Ardans as Acting Governor in 1987.

207 The newly created Kodam for the whole of Kalimantan, has its headquarters in Balikpapan. Thus, Balikpapan is replacing Banjarmasin as the capital of Kalimantan, reflecting the importance of East Kalimantan to the central government. Major General Zein Maulani is now the highest ranking Banjarese officer, only outranked by the generation of the retired Major General Hassan Basri. Most of that generation, however, has retired, including Brigadier General Firmansjah (now in the timber business) and Brigadier General M. Jusi. At the end of Governor Subardjo's term in South Kalimantan, it was difficult to find a Banjarese officer to succeed him. He was replaced by the then Commander of Lambung Mangkurat Kodam Brigadier General Mistar Tjokrokusomo, who died while in office in 1986. Mistar was replaced by Vice Governor Mohammad Said, a Banjarese official himself. Zein Maulani, who graduated first in his class of 1961 AMN graduates, has continued his military career. He was the Assistant for Operations to the Army Chief of Staff before becoming Pangdam Tanjungpura, replacing Major General Faisal Tanjung.

and provincial levels. At the top of the Golkar provincial hierarchy, the old Samarinda *pejuang*, Djunaid Sanusi, has been in a position of power since 1971. Hence, he became the key link between the various Banjarese groups within Golkar in their competition with other groups.

Other groups that have utilized Golkar and the bureaucracy in their competition for power have been the Dayak groups and the Kutai group. Two members of the MPR in 1977 were Dayak, Dra. Lun Hadaitullah and W. Ngir Wusak. Lun Hadaitullah comes from the Bahau group. In 1982 she won a DPR seat as a member of the DPR from Golkar, which she retained in the 1987 election. W. Ngir Wusak is from the Kenyah-Kayan group in the Bulungan area, and his appointment was aimed at checking the growth of the PDI within the Kenyah group under the leadership of Lentjang.[208]

The Kutai group consists mainly of lower aristocrats and people of Buginese descent, represented by the former Bupati of Kutai, Awang Faisal, and the Bupati of Kutai, Rustam Hafidz. The upper echelon of the Kutai aristocracy seems to have faded away from politics and government, although one of them, Police Brigadier General Aji Lukman Hakim has a high position at the Police Headquarters in Jakarta. Personal influence over the political process, however, is still exercised by people like A.R. Padmo, the father-in-law of Governor Ardans.

Despite the resurgence of many indigenous groups (e.g., the Banjarese, the Kenyah, the Bahau, the Kutai), East Kalimantan has been transformed into a significant national frontier region in which many ethnic groups, and power groups as well, are competing for the economic and political power that the oil, timber, and other resource exploitation activities can provide. The discovery of a 6 billion cubic meter coal deposit and of natural gas deposits in the Bontang area north of Samarinda has added to the strategic importance of East Kalimantan.[209] Not surprisingly, the chairman of the DPRD and Golkar in 1988 came from an oil-related background, having worked both at Pertamina (Indonesian Oil Company) and Total

---

208 For a short biography of Dra. Emilia Lun Hadaitullah see Biographical Appendix and **Buku MPR 1977**, p. 672.

209 It has been stated that East Kalimantan is strategically important because of, among other factors, the length of the border (about 1,000 kilometers), the depth of the Makassar Straits which could be navigated by foreign submarines, and the importance of its oil lines. (Interview with Colonel Gunadi, Kodam Mulawarman Chief of Staff, June 28, 1979.)

Indonesia, a French company. Moreover, these discoveries have fueled a further increase in the number of non-Banjarese migrants coming to East Kalimantan. This new wave of migrants is for the most part composed of Javanese migrants who can play important roles in provincial politics, given the right leadership and organization, as exemplified best by the Kodam leadership years of Soeharjo.

The rise of Muis Hassan, Wahab Sjahranie, and Ardans has demonstrated the power that the indigenous groups can wield within the particular context of East Kalimantan's provincial politics, especially with regard to its interaction with national politics. It is also in this provincial context that one can see the limits of "Javanization" in the Outer Islands as exemplified by the political constraints faced by Suharjo, Ery Supardjan, and Suwandi. Similarly, East Kalimantan's political history shows the limited and secondary role that groups such as the Kenyah, Bahau, Kutai, and Berau now must occupy in provincial politics, despite the occasional short-lived episodes of political ascendance they experienced in the past. Their rise in recent years has been facilitated by the efforts of political groups such as Golkar and PDI.

It is also evident that in a time of an increasingly powerful Indonesian military, political groups must have backing and support within the officer corps. Thus, for example, we find that the rise of Dayak groups has been encouraged by the Kodam and Ardans' gubernatorial candidacy was supported by his fellow Banjarese Pangdam of Tanjungpura and by the leadership of Golkar. Given the fact that most officers are of Javanese origin, it is likely that provincial politics in East Kalimantan will continue to be played out primarily between the Banjarese bureaucrats, the Javanese officers, and the Jakarta-connected businessmen who are mostly of Chinese descent.

BIOGRAPHICAL APPENDIX

Aji Raden Afloes

Aji Raden Afloes was born in Tenggarong in 1906 to a Kutai aristocratic family. He graduated from OSVIA Makassar in 1925 and was stationed as *Penjawat* (*camat*) in various places in Kutai. After the Revolutionary war, he was chosen as the Secretary of the Dewan Kalimantan Timur (East Borneo Council), in view of his performance representing East Borneo at the Malino Conference. He was not only instrumental in bringing East Borneo into the unitary state in April 1950, but was also appointed its first Resident. Subsequently, he was asked by the Governor of Kalimantan, Dr. Murdjani, to work as the Resident at the Governor's office in Banjarmasin. When Milono became East Kalimantan's Governor in 1956, he was appointed as the Resident of West Kalimantan. When West Kalimantan was changed into a province, he became its first Acting Governor. Because of his membership in the Masjumi party since the 1950s, he was forced to resign from the *pamong praja* in 1960 when the Masjumi party was banned. After 1960 he lived a quiet life as a businessman in Jakarta.

(Interviews with Aji Bambang Abdurrachman, Balikpapan, June 23, 1979 and Aji Raden Djokoprawiro, Malang, July 7, 1979.)

Aji Raden Mohammad Ajub

Aji Raden Mohammad Ajub was born in Gunung Tabur in 1917 where he got his "Inlandsche School" degree in 1930. Prior to 1945, he was working as a *pamong praja* in Tanjung Redeb. Between 1946 and 1950, he worked at the office of the Dewan Kalimantan Timur in Samarinda. In 1952, he was elected as Head of the Autonomous Region of Gunung Tabur and in 1960 he was appointed Bupati of Berau. He worked in this position until 1964. Subsequently he moved to Samarinda where he was an active member of the DPRD from the NU. In 1971 he was elected a member of the MPR from East Kalimantan, and in 1977 he was appointed leader of the PPP faction in the provincial branch of the DPRD.

(Interview with A.R.M. Ajub, Samarinda, June 17, 1979 and *Buku MPR 1971*, p. 764.)

Achmad Arief gelar Datoek Madjoe Orang

Achmad Arief gelar Datoek Madjoe Orang was born in August 1901 in Kamang, West Sumatra. He was the son of Tuanku Laras Tilatang. He attended HIS in Bukittinggi and OSVIA Magelang. His first job was as *kandidat ambtenar* in Batusangkar in 1921. He rose in the *pangreh praja* to become a Demang in 1940. After independence, he stayed in Bukittinggi as a Republican and refused the Dutch offer to become its *Walinagari* in Kotagedang. In 1950 he was placed in the Department of Interior in Jakarta and in 1951 was appointed Resident of East Kalimantan to replace Ruslan Muljohardjo, who in turn was appointed Governor of Central Sumatra. Datoek Madjoe Orang was the Resident of East Kalimantan until 1955. He was a candidate from PSI for the Konstituante in the 1955 election.

(This information was provided by Dr. Audrey Kahin from her field notes on West Sumatra. See also *Daftar Tjalon-tjalon Konstituante 1955* [Jakarta: Kementerian Penerangan R.I., 1955], p. 188, and Oemar Dachlan, "Perkembangan Pemerintahan Kalimantan Timur" [Samarinda: typed manuscript in author's possession, 1967], p. 6.)

Abdurrachman Aziz

Abdurrachman Aziz alias RM Noto Sunardi originally came from Balikpapan. In the early months of independence he led a *pejuang* group in Long Ikis, in the area of Pasir. He married the daughter of Long Ikis's *Wedana*. His father-in-law was killed by the Dutch. Aziz was sent to Cipinang prison in Jakarta to serve a life sentence, and he died there in 1949.

Sayid Fachrul Baraqbah

Sayid Fachrul Baraqbah was born in Tenggarong in 1925. He had just graduated from HIS Tenggarong when the Japanese occupied Indonesia. He fought as a guerrilla leader in Samarinda in late 1945 and then escaped to East Java. Fachrul took a *perahu* to East Java at a time when the Dutch dominated East Kalimantan militarily. He soon joined the *lasykar* of Pesindo in East Java and was sent to Pesindo headquarters in Yogjakarta in 1947. He became a cadre of the FDR in 1948 but survived the "Madiun Affair." He returned to Samarinda in the early 1950s to organize the provincial branch of the PKI and ran as the PKI candidate for parliament in East Kalimantan in the 1955 election. He was arrested in 1965 following the G-30-S Affair.

(Interview with Sayid Gasjim Baraqbah, Fachrul's elder brother, June 23, 1979, Samarinda.)

Aji Raden Sayid Mochsen Baraqbah

Aji Raden Sayid Mochsen Baraqbah was born in Tenggarong in 1919. He was a Kutai aristocrat of Arabic descent. His father, Aji Raden Idrus Sukmawira was a close adviser to the Sultan. He graduated from HIS Tenggarong, then went to OSVIA Makassar and graduated in 1934. He worked as *Penjawat* in the Kutai sultanate until the 1950s. After he left the office of *Penjawat* (i.e., after he left the employ of the Kutai sultanate), he was a leader of the PNI with Muis Hassan and others. When the PNI dominated the provincial bureaucracy in the early 1960s, Sayid Mochsen was a powerful figure in Samarinda and a close adviser to the Governor. He retired in 1966 with the rank of Bupati, following the anti-PNI purge after the fall of Governor Muis Hassan. In the 1970s he was active in East Kalimantan's timber business.

(Interview with his younger brother, Aji Raden Sayid Gasjim Baraqbah, June 24, 1979.)

Aji Raden Djokoprawiro

Aji Raden Djokoprawiro was born into a Kutai aristocratic family in Tenggarong in 1915. He attended HIS Tenggarong and OSVIA Makassar from which he was graduated in 1939. He later went on to AMS-B in Malang, which many aristocrats considered too out of the way at that time. He returned to Kutai after the Revolutionary war and was appointed a member of the Dewan Kalimantan Timur. As a member of the Dewan he became known as a Republican supporter. He became a member of the delegation to the Round Table Conference in The Hague in December 1949, along with Afloes, Aji Pangeran Sosronegoro, and Inche Abdul

Muis. He was appointed a member of RUSI's Senate as a representative of East Borneo. Soon afterwards he ended up with the leadership of the PIR-Hazairin. As the Parliamentary leader of the PIR-Hazairin, he not only exerted considerable influence on national politics, but was also instrumental in getting Hazairin's approval for the appointment of his fellow-PIR Kutai aristocrat, A. P. Pranoto as the first Governor. PIR's failure to secure any Parliamentary seat for East Kalimantan, however, removed him from politics. With his removal from national politics, the Kutai aristocracy lost their only representative at the national level. In the 1970s he became quite a successful businessman in the timber industry. His son, Aji Raden Rustam Effendie, is Director of Kutai Timber Indonesia Company in Jakarta. AR Djokoprawiro retired to live a quiet life in Malang.

(Interviews with Aji Raden Djokoprawiro, July 5 and 7, 1979.)

Rasjid Sutan Radja Emas

Rasjid Sutan Radja Emas was born in Bukittinggi, Minangkabau, in August 1922. He graduated from MULO in 1939 and was awarded a certificate in radio communications in 1940. His radio communications certificate enabled him to obtain a job in Tarakan in 1941 as Radio Inspector. After 1946 he became active in politics as the chairman of INI in Tarakan. He was the chairman of the Bulungan DPRD between 1948 and 1950. After 1950, he became a member of the DPRS from the PNI in Jakarta. From then on he resided in Jakarta. In 1971 he was elected a member of the MPR from the PNI. Up to 1971 he was a member of Parliament for the PNI. He was also once the head of the PNI's labor organization, KBM (Kesatuan Buruh Marhaenis).

(*Buku MPR 1971*, p. 983.)

Dra. Emilia Lun Hadaitullah

Dra. Emilia Lun Hadaitullah was born in Tering, Kutai in 1935. She graduated from IKIP Bandung. She taught at the Army's SMP (Secondary School) from 1963 to 1965. During that time she was also a member of the DPRD from Golkar. She then became a lecturer at Mulawarman University and was appointed Dean of the Social Science Faculty in 1978. She was also appointed a member of the MPR from Golkar in 1978. She was elected as a member of the DPR in 1982.

(See *Buku MPR 1977*, p. 672.)

Lieutenant Colonel R. Hartojo

Lieutenant Colonel R. Hartojo came from the Banyumas area in Central Java. He had fought the guerrillas in the Purwokerto region and was appointed Commander of Gerakan Banteng, a task force against the DI/TII, in the early 1950s. He then was sent to Egypt as Commander of Garuda I before being recalled to become the Commander of RI 22 in Balikpapan. In 1960 he was replaced as Pangdam Mulawarman by his Chief of Staff, Colonel Soeharjo. He was appointed Deputy Commander of Training and Education of the Army in Bandung. He retired as Major General in the late 1960s.

(See generally *Sejarah Kodam Muluwarman*, p. 24. Interview with Abdulmatalib, former PSI leader of East Kalimantan, who was a close associate of Hartojo at that time, conducted in Samarinda, June 22, 1979.)

Mohammad (Bob) Hasan

Mohammad (Bob) Hasan has strong ties to many of the Diponegoro officers and is said to have been adopted as a son by the late General Gatot Subroto. His concession was among those that were inspected by President Suharto from a helicopter during a visit to East Kalimantan in 1980. Bob Hasan is the chairman of the Indonesian Athletic Association. Since 1987, he has sponsored "the Bali Ten Kilometers Race" with a promised prize of up to US$ 500,000. He is also a member of the Board of the Indonesian Golf Association, while his wife, Mrs. Pertiwi Hasan, is the chairperson of the Indonesian Gymnastics Association. According to Hasyim Ning, Bob Hasan was among those that tried -- unsuccessfully -- to persuade Chaerul Saleh to support General Suharto in the critical months prior to the transfer of power from President Sukarno to General Suharto on March 11, 1966. For information on the total number of Bob Hasan's companies, see *Tempo*, September 28, 1985, pp. 64-68.

Abdul Muis Hassan

Abdul Muis Hassan was born in Samarinda into a family of second generation Banjarese migrants in June 1924. He attended MULO in Banjarmasin and returned to East Kalimantan at the end of the Japanese occupation. He became chairman of the Samarinda INI and incorporated it into the PNI in 1950, which he chaired for East Kalimantan from 1950 to 1959. Prior to his appointment as Governor of East Kalimantan in 1962, he was the head of the Social Welfare Service. He was a member of the DPRGR in Jakarta from 1960. He resigned from politics and did quite well in private business.

(Interview with Abdul Muis Hassan, July 12, 1979, Jakarta; and Dr. O. G. Roeder, *Who's Who in Indonesia* [Jakarta: Gunung Agung, 1970], pp. 502-3.)

Yulius Aloysius Husin

Yulius Aloysius Husin was born in Barongtongkok, near Long Iram, in 1937. He attended a seminary in Banjarmasin, and then graduated from a seminary in the Netherlands. He went to the Theology School in Yoyga and graduated in 1964. Upon graduation, he became a priest in Samarinda. His duties as a priest extended to the army's Kodim. In 1967 he was appointed a member of the DPRD as a representative of Golkar. He was elected in 1971 and reelected in 1977 to that position. In addition, he was elected a member of the MPR in 1971 as a Golkar representative.

(See *Buku MPR 1971*, p. 961.)

Husein Jusuf

Husein Jusuf was born in Balikpapan in 1925. He had just finished his elementary school at the time of independence. Soon thereafter he joined KIM and in 1949 was active as the Secretary of the INI Central Board. After 1950, he joined the Murba party and became its main candidate in the 1955 election. He became the chairman of the Angkatan 45 in the late 1950s and in 1959 was appointed a member of Depernas by President Sukarno. He became a member of Parliament in 1967 for Murba. In the 1971 election, however, he failed to win a parliamentary seat. After 1972, he was no longer active in East Kalimantan's politics because of the dominant political roles of PDI and Parkindo elements. He then lived in Balikpapan and led the Angkatan 45 and the Veterans' Organization with his fellow *pejuang*.

(Interviews with Husein Jusuf, June 7, 8 and 29, 1979, Balikpapan.)

Aji Raden Kariowiti

Aji Raden Kariowiti was born in Tenggarong in 1916 of a Kutai aristocratic background. He graduated from OSVIA Makassar in 1938 and worked in the Kutai bureaucracy. During the Revolution, he was the *Wedana* of Balikpapan and was sympathetic to the *pejuang*. He joined the Masjumi in the 1950s and was forced to take an early retirement in the 1960s. After his retirement, he was active in religious matters in Samarinda.

Aji Pangeran Kertanegara

Aji Pangeran Kertanegara was born in Tenggarong in 1905. He was a half-brother of Sultan Parikesit and a member of his Kutai Cabinet. He graduated from HIS Tenggarong and had studied in the Netherlands prior to the war without obtaining any degree. He was considered the most pro-Dutch of the four Cabinet members and had developed a rivalry with his pro-Republican half-brother, Pangeran Pranoto. He was appointed by Van Mook as Secretary of State Affairs of the Self-Governing Lands (Menteri Negara Urusan Swapraja) in the so-called "Interim Federal Government" of Indonesia in March 1948. After 1950, he fell entirely out of politics and government. Subsequently, he lived in Tenggarong and was in charge of the Kutai Museum.

(Interview with Kertanegara, June 20, 1979.)

Lentjang BA

Lentjang BA was born into a Kenyah family in 1937 in Long Pujungan, Bulungan. He studied at the Teachers' High School in Bandung with the support of a church fellowship. Between 1958 and 1966 he taught in the public secondary school in Tarakan. In 1967, he was appointed a member of BPH (Badan Pemerintahan Harian -- Daily Consultative Body) of Bulungan. As a member of BPH he represented the Indonesian Christian Party (Parkindo), which he chaired. In 1971, he was elected a member of Parliament from Parkindo, and in 1977 he was reelected as a member of the PDI. He was chosen as Secretary of the PDI faction in Parliament in 1978. He lost the election in 1982, but returned as a DPR member from the PDI in the 1987 election. He is now the Treasurer of the PDI faction in the DPR.

(See *Buku MPR 1977*, pp. 692-93.)

Siebold Mewengkang

Siebold Mewengkang was born in Tompasso, Minahasa, in December 1904. In 1926, after finishing secondary school (MULO) in Manado, he went to Balikpapan to work at the BPM. He worked in a BPM accounting section until he was arrested by the Dutch in 1946. He resumed his work at BPM in 1950 and established an independent labor organization there, SKBM (Sarekat Kaum Buruh Minyak -- Oil Workers Union). The SKBM was dissolved by Soeharjo in 1960. He was put in jail by Soeharjo in 1961 for about a year and was then placed under city arrest until he was released by Sumitro. He retired from the oil company in 1966 after having successfully obtained better fringe benefits for the workers.

(Interview with Siebold Mewengkang, June 28, 1979 Balikpapan.)

Dr. Mas Moerdjani

Dr. Mas Moerdjani was born in Tulungagung in 1904. He attended NIAS (Medical College) in Surabaya and graduated in 1930. While working as a doctor in Surabaya, he was also active in Dr. Sutomo's PBI. Because of his involvement in PBI activities, the Dutch removed him to Magelang and, later on, to Negara in Bali. In 1939, he moved to Bandung and set up his own medical practice. Following independence, he was first appointed Bupati of Indramayu, and later on was appointed Resident of Cirebon and Bogor. In June 1946, he became the Governor of West Java, and in January 1947 he became the Governor of East Java in Malang. In December 1949, he was given the task of persuading Sultan Hamengku Buwono IX of the need for the unification of Kalimantan into the Republic of Indonesia. He was appointed Governor of Kalimantan in Banjarmasin in February 1950. Moerdjani's appointment created an uproar among the Banjarese Republicans who demanded the return of their fellow Banjarese, Ir. Pangeran Mohammad Noor. In early 1954 he fell sick and was hospitalized in Surabaya where he died in March 1956.

(Interview with Mrs. Soeminie Moerdjanie, Jakarta, August 16, 1979.)

Aji Raden Sayid Mohammad

Aji Raden Sayid Mohammad was born into a Kutai aristocratic family of Arabic descent in Tenggarong in 1918. After graduating from OSVIA Makassar in 1940, he joined the Kutai bureaucracy. He worked there until the 1950s. He was appointed as the first mayor of Balikpapan in 1959 only to be replaced by Soeharjo's appointee, Lieutenant Colonel Bambang Sutikno. Although he had been active in the PNI in the 1960s, he was able to survive the post-1966 purge and became the deputy of Governor Wahab Sjahranie in 1970. In 1975 he retired and in 1977 he was appointed a member of the MPR from East Kalimantan, representing Golkar.

(See *Buku Daftar Riwayat Hidup Anggota MPR 1977* [Jakarta: Lembaga Pemilihan Umun, 1978], p. 670.)

Inche Abdul Muis

Inche Abdul Muis was born into a Melayu family in Samarinda in August 1920. He attended HIS, MULO, and AMS-B in Java before he was sent to study in Japan in 1943 under Japanese sponsorship. He came back to Samarinda in 1947 and became the deputy chairman of the local INI. In 1949 while a member of the Dewan Kalimantan Timur, he also led the Samarinda-based Front Nasional. In 1950 when INI was incorporated into the PNI, I. A. Muis was appointed a member of the DPRS from the PNI. He simultaneously served as a member of the DPRS and as a member of the PNI's Central Board from 1950 to 1956. In 1959 he was elected Regional Head of East Kalimantan. Less than a year later, however, he was forced to resign from this office on the grounds of fiscal mismanagement. After 1960, he became the Director of PT Pelayaran Mahakam in Jakarta. In 1970 he was elected fourth chairman of the PNI's Central Board and in 1972 he became a member of the MPR from PNI. He died in Jakarta in 1978.

(*Buku MPR 1977*, p. 991.)

Aminuddin Nata

Aminuddin Nata was born in Balikpapan in 1910. He graduated from HBS-A in Jakarta and enrolled for one year at RHS (Law School) before he went back to Balikpapan in 1945 to work in private business. While in Balikpapan, he refused a BPM offer that he work as its leading official. After independence, he led the Central Board of INI and was jailed for refusing to cooperate with the Dutch. The poor fate of the *pejuang*, and the political dominance of the Samarinda nationalists deeply troubled him. After the 1950s he retreated from political life.

(Interview with Siebold Mewengkang, June 28, 1979, Balikpapan.)

Pangeran Mohammad Noor

Mohammad Noor was born into the family of the former Banjarmasin Sultan Martapura, in South Kalimantan, in June 1901. He graduated from THS (Technical College), Bandung, in 1927. He was among the first university graduates of prewar Kalimantan. In 1931 he was appointed a member of the Volksraad from Kalimantan. He remained in that position until 1939. He then worked as an engineer until 1945. After independence, he was appointed Republican Governor for Kalimantan. He was Governor until 1950. He joined the Masjumi in 1950 and became its member in Parliament. He broke ranks with the Masjumi in 1957 when he refused to resign as Minister following the formation of the *Kabinet Kerja*. Between 1968 and 1973 he was a member of the DPA, and afterward, a member of the MPR. In 1978 he was elected a member of the DPR for South Kalimantan, where he served until his death in 1979.

(Interview with Pangeran Mohammad Noor, November 25, 1977, Jakarta and *Buku MPR 1977*, p. 64.)

Aji Raden Padmo

Aji Raden Padmo was born in Tenggarong in November 1912. He attended HIS Tenggarong and OSVIA Makassar from which he graduated in 1931. Prior to the war he worked in various positions within the Kutai sultanate, the last one as a *Penjawat* in Melak. Between 1945 and 1956, he was *Wedana* of Samarinda. Later he worked as the Bupati at the Governor's office. In 1957, he was appointed secretary to the Governor by Pranoto. He was elected Bupati of Kutai in 1960. He was arrested in 1964 by Pangdam Soeharjo and kept in prison for six months. It was only through the intervention of the then Minister of Interior, Major General Dr. Sumarno, that Soeharjo released AR Padmo in early 1965. In 1966, he was reappointed Resident of Samarinda. He was later chosen as the new Provincial Secretary by Governor Wahab Sjahranie. In 1972, he was also appointed a member of the MPR from East Kalimantan and chairman of Korpri before he retired in 1973. He then lived in Samarinda working as director of the provincial government-owned Hotels Lamin Indah.

(Interview with Aji Raden Padmo, June 25, 1979 Samarinda, and *Buku MPR 1971*, p. 763.)

Mung Parhadimuljo

Mung Parhadimuljo was born in Yogyakarta in 1923. In the 1950s he was the Commander of Regiment 18 of the Brawijaya Division. Parhadimuljo has spent most of his career in the RPKAD. In 1962 he became the Commander of the Mandala Task Force and in late 1962 he became the Commander of RPKAD. He was appointed as Pangdam Mulawarman on November 5, 1965, remaining in that position until April 1970. He then became Commander of the Army's Training for Infantry (*Pussenif Pusat Kesenjataan Infantri*). Later, he became the General Commander of the AKABRI (Indonesia Armed Forces Academy). In 1974 he was appointed Inspector General of the MABAD, and in 1977, when he reached retirement age, he was appointed as Inspector General of the Department of Agriculture.

Aji Raden Pranoto

Aji Raden Pranoto was born in Tenggarong in 1905. He graduated from OSVIA in Makassar and in 1945 was in charge of the police as a member of Kutai's Cabinet. He was considered a sympathetic advocate of the Republican cause. Early in the 1950s he joined PIR-Hazairin and with the help of AR Djokoprawirio, a fellow Kutai, he was able to work his way up to the rank of Resident in 1956. He was appointed the first Governor of East Kalimantan in 1959. By becoming a member of the NU, Pranoto was able to maintain his governorship, despite the dissolution of the PIR. However, he gave up the governorship in 1962 and soon afterwards was jailed by Soeharjo for his alleged embezzlement of government funds. He was first jailed in Balikpapan but was transferred to RTM Jakarta (Military Prison) in 1964. He died in prison, in 1966, apparently due to poor prison conditions, as a poor man, leaving a widow without a house.

(Interview with Abdul Muis Hassan, Jakarta, July 12, 1979.)

Mohammad Sabrie

Mohammad Sabrie was born in Samarinda into a Banjarese family in 1917. In 1940 he graduated from an elementary school in Tenggarong and became a teacher prior to the Japanese occupation. In 1943, he became the Commander of the BPRI guerrilla unit in Samarinda. After 1950, he became *camat* of Samarinda Seberang. He remained in that position until his appointment as a member of the DPRDGR in 1967. Later, he became the Deputy Chairman of the DPRDGR of East Kalimantan, and then its chairman. He was a member of the MPR from Golkar from 1971 until his death in 1974. Prior to 1968, he was prominent in the Murba party.

(See *Buku MPR 1971*, p. 960.)

Abdul Azis Samad

Abdul Azis Samad was born in Banjarmasin in 1922. He came to Samarinda before the war, after graduating from MULO Bandung. He was involved in INI Samarinda and Front Nasional political activities, and was appointed a member of the Dewan Kutai while in Samarinda. After 1950 he became active in the PNI and became the chairman of Kutai's DPRD. In 1957 he was elected chairman of the East Kalimantan DPRD. He served in that capacity until 1966. Afterwards he became the secretary of the Forestry Service. He retired in 1976. After the decline of the PNI in East Kalimantan, he was involved in politics. Like many PNI leaders he then became active in private business. (Interviews with Azis Samad, Samarinda, June 20 and 25, 1979.)

Abdul Wahab Sjahranie

Abdul Wahab Sjahranie was born into a Banjarese aristocratic family in Rantau, South Kalimantan. He graduated from HIS in 1937 and went to the *Bestuur Opleiding* (school for *pamong praja*) in 1941. Before independence, he worked as an employee in the Japanese occupation office. In 1947 he was appointed as *Wedana* of Kandangan. From 1947 to 1950 he worked with the famous unit of Divisi IV of ALRI under Hassan Basri. Between 1950 and 1960 he held various jobs in the army as Commander of a battalion in Kandangan, Chief of Staff of Regiment 21 Banjarmasin, and Acting Pangdam of Lambung Mangkurat, South Kalimantan. In 1961 he was appointed lecturer at SESKOAD, a year after his graduation from India's Defense Staff College. He rose to become the Head of the Infantry Department at SESKOAD. Prior to his appointment as Governor of East Kalimantan in 1967, he was Deputy to the Sixth Assistant of the Army Chief of Staff who dealt with Functional Affairs. He was the Governor of East Kalimantan from 1967 to 1978. From 1978 until his death in May 1980 he was the secretary to the Minister of State for Environment and Development Supervision. He was buried in Banjarmasin.

(See, *Buku MPR 1971*, pp. 758-59.)

Mrs. Adjang Ratminie Sjahranie

Mrs. Adjang Ratminie Sjahranie was born in the then South Kalimantan town of Kuala Kapuas in 1928. She worked as a teacher during the Japanese occupation. After independence, she was active in the Army wives' organization (Persit). In 1975, she became the deputy chairman of Golkar's Bappilu (Badan Pengendali Pemilihan Umum -- The Body to Guide the Election), an important group within Golkar. She was elected a member of Parliament representing Golkar for East Kalimantan in the general election of 1977.

(*Buku MPR 1977*, p. 650.)

R. Soeharjo

R. Soeharjo was born in Blitar in 1923. He was educated at MULO before fighting in the guerrilla war in East Java. He fought in the Kendiri-Malang-Surabaya complex during the Revolution under the leadership of the revolutionary-nationalist leader of the Brawijaya division, Colonel Bambang Supeno, with whom he maintained a close relationship. In the early Revolutionary period, he fought in the Surabaya area, cementing his hostility to the British troops. In the early 1950s, he worked at staff positions at MABAD and in the Brawijaya division. As a commander in the early 1950s, he was also instrumental in organizing the former *pejuang* in Java into a left-leaning organization, the Perbepsi (Persatuan Bekas Pejuang Seluruh Indonesia). Moreover, prior to his appointment to Balikpapan, Soeharjo had served as military aide to the visiting leader of the Democratic Republic of Vietnam, Ho Chi Minh. His short service to Ho Chi Minh further strengthened his revolutionary resolve. In 1960 he was appointed Chief of Staff of Kodam Mulawarman. He took over as Pangdam a few months later. He won the "Lumumba Award" for best direction at the Afro-Asian Film Festival held in Jakarta in late April of 1964. His film, "Tangan-Tangan Yang Kotor" [The Dirty Hands] won the Bandung Award, the highest award of the festival. In late 1964 he also became the head of the provincial leadership of the Panca Tunggal (Five Regional Bodies). He was replaced as Pangdam in March 1965 and sent to the Army Staff College in Moscow. Soeharjo returned to Indonesia in January 1977. He was detained by Kopkamtib for three years and was released in 1980. He now lives a quiet life in Jakarta. His release has mainly been attributed to the efforts of his Eurasian wife, who contacted both General Nasution and General L. B. Murdani.

(See generally *Sejarah Kodam Mulawarman*, p. 24. Interview with General Nasution, Jakarta, July 14, 1979 [for the influence of Ho Chi Minh on Soeharjo]. Interview with R. Soeharjo, Jakarta, December 17, 1984.]

Brigadier General Ery Soepardjan

Brigadier General Ery Soepardjan was born in Kutowinangun, Kebumen, Central Java in 1926. He was studying at the Technical School when the Japanese occupied Indonesia in 1942. He became Sjodancho of PETA and then the company commander of the Diponegoro Division. He retained that position until 1955. He rose to become battalion commander in 1959, and then became the Chief of Staff of Korem Yogyakarta prior to G-30-S. He had just been appointed the Inspector of Kodam III in West Sumatra when the coup occurred. After the coup he was appointed Commander of Korem Wirabumi, Riau. In 1968 he was appointed Commander of Korem 72 Yogya, and then became the Chief of Staff of Kodam Diponegoro in 1972. In 1971 he was a member of the MPR representing Yogya. In 1975 he was appointed as Pangdam Mulawarman, and in June 1978 he was appointed Governor of East Kalimantan.

(See *Sinar Harapan*, June 19, 1978 and *Buku MPR 1977*, p. 724.)

Colonel Soeparno

Colonel Soeparno was born in Kutoardjo, Central Java in 1922. He graduated from the Teacher School (HIK) in 1941 and was a teacher in Malang during the Japanese occupation. In 1945 he joined the Cadet School in Malang and then became an officer in the Army. He was mostly involved in educational institutions. In 1968 he was appointed Chief of Staff of Kodam Mulawarman. During this time he was also the chairman of Golkar for East Kalimantan. He was a member of the MPR for East Kalimantan from 1971 until his transfer to Surabaya to become the new mayor of that city. He was not reelected as mayor in 1978, possibly because of opposition from the Governor of East Java, Sunandar Prijosudarmo. Though his name was raised as a possible candidate for Governor of East Kalimantan, that appointment never materialized.

(See *Buku MPR 1977*, pp. 760-61.)

Siel Stekanggen

Siel Stekanggen was born in 1930 in the same town where Mrs. Adjang Sjahranie was born, Kuala Kapuas, Kalimantan. He attended an agricultural school, and then the preparatory school, Kursus Dinas (KDC). He was a member of the Army between 1950 and 1953, and later became an employee at the Governor's office in Samarinda. In 1965, he was appointed *camat* Loah Janan for Kutai. He became the deputy chairman of the DPRD of East Kalimantan, representing IPKI, in 1967. He then joined Golkar in 1970 and became its MPR member in 1971.

(See, *Buku MPR 1971*, p. 962.)

W. Ngir Wusak

W. Ngir Wusak was born in Kerayan, Bulungan, in 1933. He went to secondary school in 1953 and worked in Sarawak, Malaysia, from 1953 to 1957. He was also active as a Bible School teacher in Kerayan until 1969. In 1971 he joined Golkar and was appointed a member of the MPR in 1977.

GLOSSARY OF ABBREVIATIONS

AKABRI   Akademi Angkatan Bersenjata Republik Indonesia (Indonesian Armed Forces Academy); a joint academy of the three armed forces services and the police, founded in 1966.

ALRI   Angkatan Laut Republik Indonesia (Indonesian Navy).

AMN   Akademi Militer Nasional (National Military Academy), founded in 1957 in Magelang and changed to become the Army part of AKABRI, in 1966.

AMS   Algemene Middelbare School (General High School).

APT   Aji Pangeran Tumenggung, a noble title reserved for brothers of Sultans of Kutai who were appointed as the Sultans' advisers.

Baperki   Badan Permusjawaratan Kewarganegaraan Indonesia (the Body for Cooperation of Indonesian Citizenship); an organization of mostly Indonesians of Chinese descent.

Bappeda   Badan Perencana Pembangunan Daerah (the Planning Agency for Regional Development).

BB   Binnenlands Bestuur; Interior Administration in the Dutch colonial period.

BFO   Bijeenkomst voor Federaal Overleg (Federal Consultative Committee); association of Dutch-supported states in Revolutionary period.

BPM   Bataafsche Petroleum Maatschappij ([Dutch] Batavia Oil Company).

BPRI	Badan Pemberontak Republik Indonesia (the Rebel Militia for Indonesian Republic).
Depernas	Dewan Perancang Nasional (National Planning Council); a planning agency under a noted historian, Professor Yamin, in the late 1950s.
Dirjen	Direktur Jenderal (Director General); the equivalent of Assistant Secretary.
DI/TII	Darul Islam/Tentara Islam Indonesia (Land of Islam/ Indonesian Islamic Army); the unified symbol of various rebellions in West Java, Aceh, Sulawesi, and Central Java in the 1950s and early 1960s.
Ditjen	Direktorat Jenderal (Directorate General); sub-departmental level.
DPA	Supreme Advisory Council; the body to advise the President according to the 1945 Constitution.
DPD	Dewan Pemerintah Daerah (Regional Executive Council); the powerful regional body in the 1950s.
DPRD	Dewan Perwakilan Rakyat Daerah (Regional People's Representative Council).
DPRDGR	Dewan Perwakilan Rakyat Daerah Gotong Royong (Mutual Cooperation DPR), established in 1960.
dr.	Dokter (medical doctor).
drs.	doktorandus (university graduates).
Dwikora	Dwi Komando Rakyat (People's Two Commands); President Sukarno's anti-Malaysia commands in the early 1960s.
Foni	Fonds National Indonesia (Indonesian National Funds); a Republican movement in East Kalimantan in the late 1940s.
Gapi	Gaboengan Politik Indonesia (Indonesian Political Association); a federation of nationalist movements in the prewar period.
G-30-S	Gerakan 30 September (the 30 September Movement); a movement that attempted a coup on October 1, 1965, under Lieutenant Colonel Untung.

GMNI	Gerakan Mahasiswa Nasional Indonesia (Indonesian National Student Movement); a student organization of the Indonesian National Party; since 1975 it has become an independent student movement.
Golkar	Golongan Karya (Functional Group); the political organization under the sponsorship of the Army; established in 1968 but originating from the old Joint Secretariat of Functional Groups, founded in 1964.
H.	Haji; a honorary title for Moslems who have made the pilgrimage to Mecca.
Hankam	Departemen Pertahanan dan Keamanan (Department of Defense and Security).
HAMD	Himpunan Anggota Masyarakat Dompu (the Association of Dompu's Society); a voluntary association of the people of Dompu and Sumbawa, in Jakarta.
HBS	Hoogere Burger School (Citizens' High School); an elite high school in the colonial period.
HIS	Hollands Inlandsche School (Dutch Native School); an elementary school for Indonesian children conducted primarily in Dutch.
HMI	Himpunan Mahasiswa Islam (Islamic Student Association); the largest Islamic student movement since the 1950s.
HPH	Hak Pengusahaan Hutan (Forest Concession Rights); Forestry Rights License.
IHH	Iuran Hasil Hutan (Royalty Fee from Forest Products).
IHHT	Iuran Hasil Hutan Tambahan (Additional Royalty from Forest Products).
IHPH	Iuran Hak Pengusahaan Hutan (License Fee from the Rights to Exploit the Forest).
IKIP	Institut Keguruan dan Ilmu Pendidikan (the Institute for Teachers).
Inhutani	Industri Hutan Negara Indonesia (Indonesian State Forest Industry); a state enterprise for forest exploitation, founded in 1973.

INI	Ikatan Nasional Indonesia (Indonesian National Association); a Republican movement in East Kalimantan in the late 1940s.
Ipeda	Iuran Pembangunan Daerah (Regional Development Tax); tax from landholding.
Ir.	Insinyur (engineer).
ITCI	International Timber Corporation Indonesia; a big company in forest exploitation in East Kalimantan.
Kadin	Kamar Dagang dan Industri (Indonesian Chamber of Commerce and Industry).
KAMI	Kesatuan Aksi Mahasiswa Indonesia (Indonesian Student Action United Group); a student federation in the post-G-30-S period.
KAPPI	Kesatuan Aksi Pemuda Pelajar Indonesia (Indonesian Secondary School Students and Youth United Group); a federation of organizations of secondary schools' students in the post-G-30-S period.
Kasdam	Kepala Staf Komando Daerah Militer (Chief of Staff of the Regional Military Command).
Kaskarda	Kepala Staf Kekaryaan Daerah (Chief of Staff of the Regional Functional Task).
KIM	Komite Indonesia Merdeka (Committee for Indonesian Independence).
Kingmi	Kongres Injil Gereja Masehi Indonesia (Congregation of Indonesian Protestant Church); a Christian congregation with a strong presence in East Kalimantan's Dayak population.
KNIL	Koninklijk Nederlands Indisch Leger (Royal Netherlands Indies Army).
Kodam	Komando Daerah Militer (Regional Military Command).
Korem	Komando Resort Militer (Resort Military Command, covering small provinces).
Kodim	Komando Distrik Militer (District Military Command, covering the whole *kabupaten*).

Kopkamtib	Komando Pemelihara Keamanan dan Ketertiban (the Command to Maintain Order and Security).
Korpri	Korps Pegawai Republik Indonesia (the Association of the Employees of the Indonesian State, founded in 1972 as a federation of all organizations of the state's employees).
Kostrad	Komando Strategis Angkatan Darat (Army's Strategic Command).
KPMKT	Keluarga Pelajar Mahasiswa Kalimantan Timur (the Association of East Kalimantan's Students); a federation of East Kalimantan students in Java.
KKK	Kerukunan Keluarga Kalimantan (Association of Kalimantan People); a voluntary association of people from Kalimantan in Jakarta.
KRTP	Kayan River Timber Products; a larger timber company in East Kalimantan.
Laksus Kopkamtibda	Pelaksana Khusus Komando Pemelihara Keamanan dan Ketertiban Daerah (Special Holder of the Regional Command to Maintain Order and Security).
Mabad (MBAD)	Markas Besar Angkatan Darat (Central Command of the Army).
Masjumi	Madjelis Sjuro Muslimin Indonesia (Council of Indonesian Moslem Association); originally founded as a federation of Islamic organizations during the Japanese occupation and changed into a political party in 1945. It was banned in 1960.
MPR	Majelis Permusyawaratan Rakyat (People's Consultative Assembly); the body that was empowered by the 1945 Constitution to elect the President.
NIAS	Nederlandsche Indische Arts School (School of Medicine of the Netherlands Indies); a prewar medical school in Surabaya.
NIT	Negara Indonesia Timur (East Indonesian State); a Dutch-created state during the Federal period.
NV	Limited Company.

NU	Nahdhatul Ulama (Association of Islamic Scholars); an organization of Islamic scholars, founded in 1926, which became a party in 1953.
OSVIA	Opleiding School voor Inlandsche Ambtenaren (Training Schools for Native Officials).
Pangab	Panglima Angkatan Bersenjata (Commander of the Armed Forces).
Pangdak	Panglima Daerah Angkatan Kepolisian (Regional Commander of the Police).
Pangdam	Panglima Daerah Militer (Regional Military Commander); commander of the army's regional command.
Parindra	Partai Indonesia Raya (Great Indonesia's Party); a nationalist party in the prewar period up to the 1950s.
PBI	Partai Bangsa Indonesia (Indonesian National Party) a nationalist party in the prewar period.
PDI	Partai Demokrasi Indonesia (Indonesian Democratic Party); a party that emerged from the enforced merger of all non-Islamic parties in 1972.
Pepelrada	Pembantu Pelaksana Dwikora Daerah (the Regional Holder of the Dwikora Command); a power of martial law in several regions between 1963 and 1967.
Perbum	Persatuan Buruh Minyak (Association of Oil Workers); an organization of oil workers under the Indonesian Communist Party, in the 1950s and up to 1965.
Perhutani	Perusahaan Hutan Negara Indonesia (Indonesian State Forest Company); with exploitation areas only in Java.
PIR-H	Partai Indonesia Raya-Hazairin (Hazairin faction of Great Indonesia's Party); a nationalist party in the 1950s; with bases in the Outer Islands.
PKI	Partai Komunis Indonesia (Indonesian Communist Party); banned in 1966.
PNI	Partai Nasional Indonesia (Indonesian National Party); a nationalist party first founded in 1927. It was merged into the impotent PDI in 1972.

PNN	Perusahaan Niaga Negara (State Trading Corporation).
PPP (P3)	Partai Persatuan Pembangunan (Development United Party); a party that was born from enforced merger of all Islamic parties by the government in 1972.
PSI	Partai Sosialis Indonesia (Indonesian Socialist Party); a social-democratic leaning party that was banned in 1960.
PSII	Partai Sjarikat Islam Indonesia (the Party of Islamic Union of Indonesia); first originated from Sarekat Islam of the 1920s and was merged into P3 in 1972.
PT	Perseroan Terbatas (Limited Company).
RPKAD	Resimen Para Komando Angkatan Darat (the Regiment of the Army's Paratroops); a famous "red Beret" striking force of the Army.
RTM	Rumah Tahanan Militer (Military Detention Center); a famous military prison on Budi Utomo street, Jakarta, which mostly housed political prisoners.
RUSI	Republican Union of States of Indonesia.
Sekwilda	Sekretaris Wilayah Daerah (Provincial Secretary); the next-ranking official in the regional government after the Governor and the Bupati.
SH	Sarjana Hukum; a title for those who have graduated from the Faculty of Law.
Skarda	Staf Kekaryaan Daerah (Regional Staff for Functional Affairs); the officers in charge of political affairs in the Kodam.
Skarwil	Staf Kekaryaan Wilayah (Regional Staff for Functional Affairs); the officers in charge of social-political affairs in the Kowilhan.
SKB	Serikat Kaum Buruh (Association of Laborers); an association of oil workers in the early 1950s in East Kalimantan.
SKBM	Serikat Kaum Buruh Minyak (Association of Oil Workers); an independent oil workers union in the 1950s in East Kalimantan and Sumatra.

SKI	Serikat Kerakyatan Indonesia (Indonesian People's Association); a local party in South Kalimantan in the revolutionary period with additional strength in North Sumatra in the 1950s.
S S K A D - SESKOAD	Sekolah Staff dan Komando Angkatan Darat (Army Staff College). SSKAD in the 1950s, after the 1960s became SESKOAD.
TNI	Tentara Nasional Indonesia (Indonesian National Army); the formal name of the Indonesian armed forces.
TT	Tentara dan Territorium (Army and Territorial Command); division of the Army's regional commands before the reorganization in 1958.
UI	Universitas Indonesia (University of Indonesia); in Jakarta.
Unmul	Universitas Mulawarman (Mulawarman University); in Samarinda.
Untag	Universitas 17 Agustus 1945 (University of 17th of August 1945); a PNI-run university in various cities, with the center in Jakarta.
Wapangab	Wakil Panglima Angkatan Bersenjata (Deputy Commander of the Armed Forces); a new post that was created in 1970 to balance the powerful post of Pangab (and Minister of Defense).

INDEX

East Kalimantan: The Decline of a Commercial Aristocracy
is indexed by Google Books.
Kindly visit http://books.google.com to search the full text.

www.ingramcontent.com/pod-product-compliance
Lightning Source LLC
Chambersburg PA
CBHW020003290326
41935CB00007B/281